Leadership Implementation Guide

Supporting *READ 180* in Your District

Dear *READ 180* Leader,

Welcome to the *READ 180 Leadership Implementation Guide.*

This guide is written for you, a district leader, because our experience demonstrates
that district leadership is an essential component of a successful intervention program.
Our goal is to ensure that you have an overview of all the tools and strategies necessary to
implement *READ 180* successfully and to help students "do a 180" in their reading abilities.

Have you ever seen a student "do a 180?" It's a complete turn around. Understanding
replaces confusion. Confidence replaces embarrassment. Motivation replaces frustration.
Success replaces failure. *READ 180* is a research-based reading intervention program
designed to raise the reading levels and test scores of struggling readers in Grades 3
through 12. *READ 180* is the answer to the number one problem in education today:
older students reading below grade level.

For struggling students, the inability to read and write often results in other problems
with behavior, truancy, and failure. Extensive research with thousands of students has
shown that *READ 180* is dramatically effective in restoring students' self-esteem and
getting them back on track to reading at grade level.

This *Leadership Implementation Guide* will provide you with all the resources and
information necessary to return to your district and begin implementing *READ 180*
effectively. Throughout this guide, you will be introduced to all components of the
READ 180 program and learn how the components work together to provide individually
adjusted instruction for all students. You will learn how *READ 180* directly addresses
individual needs through customized instructional software, high-interest literature,
and systematic direct instruction in reading skills, vocabulary, writing, and grammar.

We on the *READ 180* team thank you for your dedication to helping struggling readers
become successful readers.

Sincerely,

Ernest B. Fleishman
Senior Vice President, Education and Corporate Relations
Scholastic Inc.

Table of Contents

Understanding *READ 180* Research and Results

READ 180 is built on more than two decades of scientifically based research and the collaboration of reading experts. Developed in clinical and classroom settings, *READ 180* brings together the essential building blocks of effective reading intervention to break the cycle of failure, accelerate instruction, and allow struggling readers to experience success.

- **The Six Components of Successful Reading Intervention**
- **The History of *READ 180***
- **Scientifically Based Research on *READ 180***
- **Teaching Foundations**
- **The *READ 180* Logic-of-Change Model**

The Six Components of Successful Reading Intervention

READ 180 is an intensive reading intervention program designed to meet the needs of students whose reading achievement is below the proficient level. The program directly addresses individual needs through adaptive and instructional software, high-interest literature, and direct instruction in reading and writing skills.

To truly succeed, a systematic program of reading intervention must incorporate six crucial elements. By bringing together the essential building blocks of effective intervention, *READ 180* breaks the cycle of failure, accelerates instruction, and allows struggling readers to experience success.

1. Scientific Research Base

The scientific development of *READ 180* began in 1985 when Dr. Ted Hasselbring of Vanderbilt University developed breakthrough software that used student performance data to individualize, adjust, and differentiate the path of reading instruction. Research continued through the 1990s as it was put to the test in Florida's Orange County public school system (See pages 4 to 5).

2. Proven Results

READ 180 is proven to work. Students who enter the program unable to read consistently experience success and become readers. After ten years of research in association with Vanderbilt University and over six years in schools, *READ 180* has brought significant gains in reading proficiency for the students who need it most (See pages 6 to 9).

3. Comprehensive Instruction

READ 180 includes a teaching system that equips—and trains—educators to deliver effective reading, writing, and vocabulary instruction to struggling readers. Teachers receive a rich and engaging curriculum of skills instruction, point-of-use professional development, a variety of assessment tools, and reports that link to resources for differentiating instruction (See pages 16 to 17).

4. Purposeful Assessment

READ 180 gives you the power to track and analyze student performance throughout the program. A variety of instruments accurately assess students to identify their most urgent needs, enabling the program and teacher to adjust instruction accordingly (see pages 75 to 82).

5. Data-Driven Instruction

READ 180 is the only program of its kind that uses assessment data so effectively to differentiate instruction. The *READ 180* Software continually adjusts the level of instruction based on student performance. Actionable reports and periodic checkpoints alert teachers to students' needs and direct them to resources for individualizing instruction (see pages 32 to 34).

6. Comprehensive Professional Development

Scholastic has designed a comprehensive professional development solution which includes implementation trainings, in-person seminars throughout the school year, an online course, and teaching materials that integrate professional development to provide educators with the background, teaching routines, and instructional support they need, when they need it (see pages 67 to 74).

The History of *READ 180*

READ 180 is built on more than two decades of scientifically based research and the collaboration of reading experts. Developed in clinical and classroom settings, the program is uniquely positioned to address the needs of struggling readers.

Early Research

Continuous Research, Testing, and Development

1985	1994–1996	1997	1998

1985

Research by **Dr. Ted Hasselbring** of Vanderbilt University leads to a **breakthrough prototype** for software that uses individual student performance data to differentiate reading instruction. This research was partially funded by a grant from the Office of Special Education, U.S. Department of Education.

1994–1996

Dr. Hasselbring joins forces with Dr. Janet Allen of the University of Central Florida, and Florida's Orange County public school system to create the **Orange County Literacy Project** for its lowest-performing students. The project uses the **Vanderbilt software** as part of a larger program of reading intervention. The project's instructional model, rooted in research-proven literacy practices, becomes the basis of the *READ 180* **Instructional Model**.

1997

Scholastic enters into collaboration with Orange County schools and Vanderbilt University to replicate the best practices of their research in a published program. *READ 180* adopts the **Lexile Framework**®, developed by **Dr. Jack Stenner** of MetaMetrics, Inc., as its leveling system. This framework provides a common metric for measuring text difficulty and student reading level.

1998

Dr. David Rose of Harvard University and his team at the Center for Applied Special Technologies develop **Universal Access capabilities** for the developing program.

Research and Implementation

Implementation and Validation

1998–1999

1999

2002–2004

2004–2005

The Council of Great City Schools pilots *READ 180* in some of its largest urban schools and enters into a research partnership to study the efficacy of the program.

Scholastic publishes *READ 180*, which is immediately implemented in hundreds of schools nationwide.

READ 180 has been the subject of continuous scientific research since its inception. The results are consistent. Students reveal significant growth on multiple measures of reading comprehension. For sites where comparison groups are available, the performance for students in *READ 180* is significantly greater than that of comparison groups. Furthermore, *READ 180* results reveal significant learning gains made across subgroups including **English-Language Learners, Special Education students, African-American students, and Native American students**.

Through continued collaboration with **Dr. Ted Hasselbring** and a new partnership with **Dr. Kevin Feldman** and **Dr. Kate Kinsella**, Scholastic launches ***READ 180 Enterprise Edition***. This new edition brings together five years of experience observing best practices in the classroom and the knowledge of experts in the field of adolescent literacy to provide an even more effective reading intervention solution.

Scientifically Based Research on *READ 180*

READ 180 is currently in use in more than 6,000 classrooms nationwide, and is one of the most thoroughly researched and documented reading intervention programs. After over a decade of research in association with Vanderbilt University and six years in schools, *READ 180* is producing quantifiable gains in reading achievement.

Closing the Achievement Gap Nationwide

A third-party efficacy study was undertaken by Interactive Inc. on behalf of the Council of Great City Schools and Scholastic. In this study, students using *READ 180* in Boston, Dallas, and Columbus were measured using the SAT-9 for reading and Normal Curve Equivalent (NCE) score expression. For the 2000–2001 school year, *READ 180* students showed increases in their reading scores of 2.8, 4.9, and 1.7 NCEs, respectively. In each case, students using *READ 180* showed statistically significant improvement in reading scores, with average NCE gains at least double those of equivalent control groups.

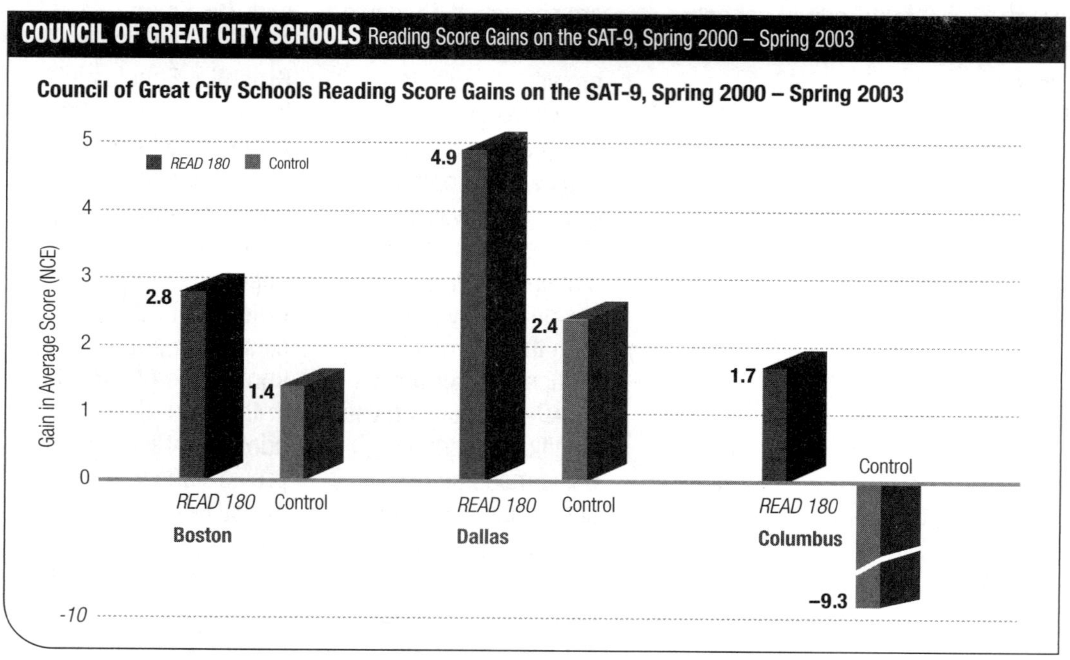

For the 2000–2001 school year, *READ 180* students showed at least double the improvement of equivalent control groups.

Proven Results for AYP Student Groups

Research has shown the effectiveness of *READ 180* in meeting the needs of struggling readers across AYP demographic groups. The following table outlines key *READ 180* features that address instructional needs of specific student groups.

Demographic Groups	*READ 180* Features	Scientifically Based Research Studies
English-Language Learners	• **Context-relevant vocabulary** accelerates language acquisition. • **Mental model development** builds background knowledge and improves comprehension. • **Multicultural materials** are engaging and relevant. • **Language support** is available in five languages for key words and video.	• *READ 180* English-Language Learners Impact Study • Los Angeles Unified School District Effectiveness Report • Impact Study: Compilation of School Studies
Special Education	• **Universal access features** enable students with certain physical disabilities to access the program. • **Multi-model materials** ensure that all students benefit. • **Motivational software** enables students to work at their own pace in a supportive environment.	• *READ 180* Special Education Impact Study • *READ 180* Middle Schools Effectiveness Reports from Des Moines, Iowa • Impact Study: Compilation of School Studies
Free and Reduced Lunch	• **Adaptive, instructional software** individualizes instruction and accelerates learning. • **Continuous assessment and dynamic reports** facilitate differentiated instruction. • **High-interest, leveled paperbacks** build fluency, vocabulary, and comprehension.	• Council of Great City Schools *READ 180* Effectiveness Report • Los Angeles Unified School District Effectiveness Report • Impact Study: Compilation of School Studies
Racial Groups (African-Americans, Asian/Pacific Islanders, Caucasians, Hispanics, and Native Americans)	• **Multicultural materials** are engaging and relevant. • **Adaptive, instructional software** individualizes instruction and accelerates learning. • **Dynamic reports** facilitate differentiated instruction. • **High-interest, leveled paperbacks** build fluency, vocabulary, and comprehension.	• *READ 180* Effectiveness Report • Los Angeles Unified School District Effectiveness Report • *READ 180* Compilation of School Studies • Impact Study: Compilation of School Studies

See the ***READ 180* Placement, Assessment, and Reporting Guide** for recommended reports.

English-Language Learners

READ 180 has been proven to raise the reading achievement scores of English-Language Learners. Special features in the program are especially helpful to students who are learning English as a second language, enabling them to master critical reading skills.

Special Features

- *READ 180* Topic Software and **rBook**™ Anchor Videos build background knowledge and help students develop mental models.

- Text captioning allows students to read along with examples of modeled fluent reading.

- *READ 180* Software provides opportunities for repeated oral reading practice, including making recordings.

- Language support is provided in Spanish, Cantonese, Vietnamese, Hmong, and Haitian Creole through video summaries and word translations.

- Spanish pronunciation tips help students decode and recognize English sounds.

- Multicultural content makes the program relevant to students from diverse backgrounds.

- Oral language development and strategies are integrated into the teaching materials.

Results

In the 2000–2001 school year, an independent research study of *READ 180* was conducted in the Los Angeles Unified School District. A group of 536 students not participating in any special intervention, matched on pretest means, gender, ethnicity, and language proficiency, was chosen for comparison data.

Using *READ 180* helped the experimental group of students make significant progress in reading over the course of one school year. The comparison group actually experienced a loss both in Reading and Language Arts.

Analysis of the disaggregated data showed that 69% of the participants were noted as Limited English Proficient (LEP) or had been recently reclassified from LEP. The gains of these students were essentially identical to the entire *READ 180* group.

Videos build background knowledge and mental models, improving reading comprehension.

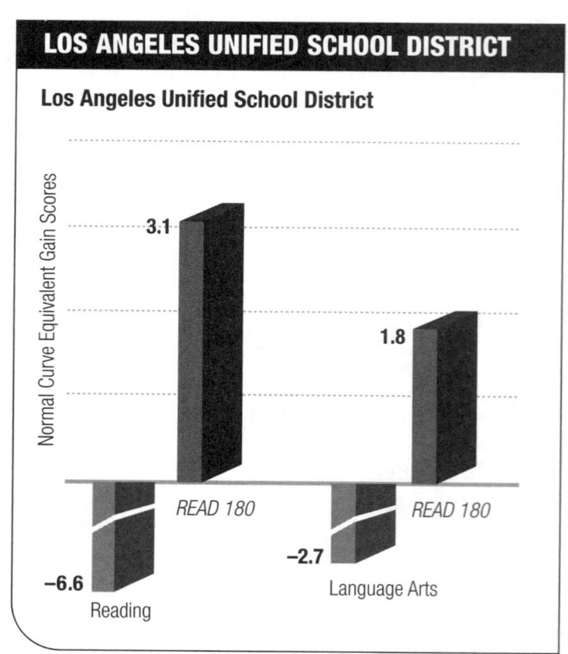

READ 180 provides support in the following languages:
- Spanish
- Cantonese
- Hmong
- Vietnamese
- Haitian Creole

Special Education Students

Many students are placed in Special Education programs because they never learned to read. *READ 180* is proven effective in accelerating reading achievement for all students— including those in Special Education.

Special Features

- Universal design features enable students with certain physical disabilities to access the text.

- Multimodal curriculum ensures that all students will benefit.

- Adaptive software and Small-Group Instruction allow for students to progress at their own pace and receive individualized instruction.

- The Instructional Model and high-interest materials keep students motivated and engaged.

Adaptive software individualizes instruction for each student.

Leaving No Students Behind

An effectiveness study by the research department at the Des Moines Independent Community School District was conducted to determine to what degree *READ 180* accelerates reading performance for 6th, 7th, and 8th grade Special Education students. The study analyzed performance results of 300 students in Special Education in the 2000–2001 school year and 160 students in the 2001–2002 school year. The Stanford Diagnostic Reading Test (SDRT), a norm-referenced assessment, was one of the instruments used in the study.

18% of students placed out of Special Education services for reading after using *READ 180* during the 2001–2002 school year.

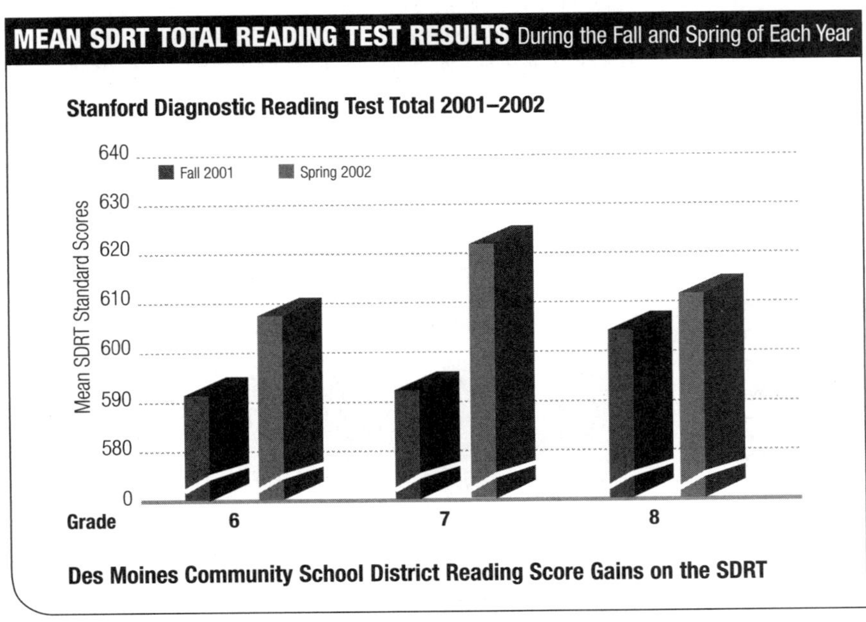

Teaching Foundations

READ 180 helps educators meet the accountability requirements of the No Child Left Behind act (NCLB). The legislation states that five essential elements must be part of an effective reading program: phonemic awareness, phonics, fluency, vocabulary, and text comprehension.

PHONEMIC AWARENESS	PHONICS	FLUENCY	VOCABULARY
"Phonemic awareness instruction helps children learn to read, spell, and comprehend text." (NCLB)	**"Systematic and explicit phonics instruction significantly improves reading comprehension." (NCLB)**	**"Fluency develops as a result of many opportunities to practice reading with a high degree of success." (NCLB)**	**"Direct instruction of vocabulary related to text leads to better comprehension." (NCLB)**
• The *READ 180* Software provides individualized phonemic awareness training based on the assessed needs of each student. • Phonemic awareness activities reinforce core skills such as sound identification and matching, phoneme blending, phoneme segmentation, and phoneme manipulation.	• A complete phonics scope and sequence is embedded in the Software to provide intense and differentiated phonics practice and instruction. As students work, the Software continually collects data on their word-recognition proficiency and adjusts instruction. • Instruction is provided through decoding tips with modeled practice in segmenting, blending, structural analysis, and correct pronunciation. • As students engage in intensive practice of study words, previously mastered study words and patterns are systematically reviewed. • The Topic Software provides pronunciation tips that are specifically geared to the needs of Spanish-speaking students to target common areas of difficulty relating to sound-symbol correspondence and pronunciation. • As students receive individualized instruction and practice in phonics and word recognition, the *Scholastic Achievement Manager* (SAM) continually collects data and reports on student progress. SAM links teachers to appropriate electronic resources for further instruction and practice.	• *READ 180* Software builds automaticity and fluency at the word and passage levels through individualized reading practice and instruction. • The Topic Software provides continuous, scaffolded practice and a wealth of opportunities for repeated reading of leveled text. • The Paperback and Audiobook libraries provide leveled books that present age-appropriate, motivating text that students can read with success to build fluency. • The *Placement, Assessment, and Reporting Guide* provides an Oral Fluency Assessment for fluency progress monitoring. • Leveled fluency practice passages and fluency routines provide materials for frequent practice.	• The *READ 180 rBook* presents high-utility vocabulary taught through a research-based teaching routine that promotes understanding and use of words that students will encounter in all content areas. • Recursive vocabulary in *rBook* reading selections promotes frequent review, practice, and reinforcement. • Activities in the *rBook* build academic language through the use of sentence starters and frequent opportunities to engage in academic discourse with support. • Vocabulary and word-study instruction is linked to data collected by the *Scholastic Achievement Manager*. Materials for targeted instruction and guided practice of vocabulary and word-study skills are available both electronically and in *Resources for Differentiated Instruction*. • All words in the Topic Software are defined and key words are translated into Spanish, Cantonese, Hmong, Haitian Creole, and Vietnamese.

<table>
<tr><th>TEXT COMPREHENSION</th><th>SPELLING</th><th colspan="2">WRITING AND GRAMMAR</th></tr>
<tr>
<td>"Text comprehension can be improved by instruction that helps readers use specific comprehension strategies." (NCLB)</td>
<td>Struggling readers have fewer experiences with text and need more direct instruction and structured support to develop spelling knowledge.</td>
<td colspan="2">As students develop basic writing skills, shared and modeled writing supports them as they face the challenges of generating and organizing their thoughts on paper.</td>
</tr>
</table>

TEXT COMPREHENSION

- The Software and *rBook* Anchor Videos help build the background knowledge that struggling readers commonly need in order to be able to construct meaning. These motivating videos help students build mental models as they read to promote text comprehension.

- The *rBook* presents intensive, systematic, and explicit instruction in essential comprehension skills and strategies. Instruction focuses on key skills for extended periods to promote application.

- Ongoing, curriculum-based assessment of comprehension is linked to materials for additional practice, review, and reteaching both electronically through the *Scholastic Achievement Manager* and in *Resources for Differentiated Instruction*.

- Topic Software continually assesses students' comprehension skills and builds mastery through higher-level thinking activities that promote strategic application of skills.

SPELLING

- The *READ 180* Software presents spelling instruction and practice that is assessment-based and individualized for each student. Spelling errors are addressed with immediate, corrective feedback.

- Spelling activities on the Topic Software continually assess students' proficiency and collect data on their most common errors.

- Spelling data is reported through the *Scholastic Achievement Manager* and is linked to resources for additional practice and review, available both electronically through the *Scholastic Achievement Manager* and in *Resources for Differentiated Instruction*.

WRITING AND GRAMMAR

- The *READ 180 rBook* presents writing in the service of reading. Writing and grammar instruction is integrally linked to reading through content, text structure, and vocabulary.

- The *rBook* scaffolds instruction for struggling writers through research-based techniques, including the use of graphic organizers, sentence starters, and writing frames. Through consistent use of these scaffolds, students are guided to internalize common organizational structures and conventions of writing.

- The *READ 180 rBook* presents carefully scaffolded instruction of the key types of writing: narrative, descriptive, expository, and persuasive. Functional (technical) writing and literary response are also included.

- Writing is assessed through multiple modes, including rubrics for self- and peer assessment, teacher assessment, and curriculum-embedded *rSkills Tests*. Assessment is linked to materials for additional instruction and practice available electronically through the *Scholastic Achievement Manager* and in *Resources for Differentiated Instruction*.

- Writing instruction and practice follows the writing process and includes frequent opportunities for timed writing practice that build readiness for the on-demand writing required on standardized assessments.

- *READ 180* materials integrate grammar, usage, and mechanics instruction based on common errors within the context of writing.

- Students are guided to write for specific purposes and audiences. Writing is shared through peer feedback and a variety of publishing opportunities.

The *READ 180* Logic-of-Change Model

This chart shows the *READ 180* Logic-of-Change Model. This model represents a conceptual overview of how the program is intended to work, the resources required to make it effective, and the outcomes that you can expect your students to reach. Only when the conditions in these two columns are met can you expect growth in reading skills and improvements in students' attitudes and behaviors.

RESOURCES/IMPACTS

- Teacher professional development

- Networked computers with microphones and headsets and teacher workstations

- Time set aside in a 90-minute block for instruction 5 days per week

- CD players with headsets

- Audiobooks, Paperbacks, Topic Software for *READ 180*

- Classroom size and arrangement adequate for *READ 180* instruction

ONGOING TEACHING/LEARNING ACTIVITIES

- 20 minutes Whole-Group Instruction to start the class

- Teachers regularly use *READ 180* instructional strategies and materials contained in *READ 180* program guides

- Small-group rotations—Students divided into 3 groups each spending 20 minutes rotating through:

    Small-Group Instruction

    Modeled and Independent Reading

    Instructional Software

- 10 minutes of Whole-Group Wrap-Up to conclude the class

- Teachers and administrators regularly use diagnostic tests (SRI) and *Scholastic Achievement Manager* for continuous assessment, placement, and monitoring

SHORT-TERM OUTCOMES

- Improved reading skills
- Improved classroom behavior
- Increased motivation

LONG-TERM OUTCOMES

- Increased scores on achievement tests
- Increased school attendance rate
- Decreased disciplinary incidents
- Improved learning in all subject areas

Contextual effects such as the characteristics of the school district, other instructional programs in use, and external events.

READ 180 Logic-of-Change Model

The first two columns form the framework for research that can be used to assess implementation. The two columns on the right side of the model illustrate the types of outcomes that you can expect from *READ 180*. The order in which the columns appear and the direction of the arrows connecting them suggest a causal chain for the outcomes you can expect from *READ 180*. The first step in implementing the program is to ensure that all of the necessary resources are in place. The second step is to see that all of the teaching and learning activities actually occur. Both steps are essential for students to reap maximum benefits from *READ 180*.

Only when the conditions in the first two columns are met can you expect growth in reading skills and improvements in students' attitudes and behaviors. For example, if *READ 180* is implemented fully in the early fall, about the time that classes begin, and students engage in *READ 180* instructional activities over a 14-week period, some indicators of progress should begin to appear. The longer students are in the program, the more their outcomes should accrue. However, the rate of these increases is almost certain to vary with the quality of program implementation, especially the amount of time allocated for *READ 180*. Scholastic strongly recommends that students remain in the program for at least one school year. Based on experience and anecdotal reports from teachers and others who are familiar with *READ 180*, you should expect to see other improvements. Even small classroom successes for students who have been struggling may result in changes in motivation, attitudes toward school, behavior, and attendance.

Using the *READ 180* Program Components

READ 180 directly addresses individual needs through adaptive and instructional software, high-interest texts, and direct instruction in reading skills. The teaching system includes comprehensive instructional materials for Whole- and Small-Group Instruction, assessment tools, and materials for differentiated instruction.

- **Teacher and Student Materials**
- **Targeted Skills Instruction**
- **Differentiated Instruction**
- **Topic Software Content**
- **Data-Driven Instruction**
- **Shared Reading With the *READ 180 rBook***

Teacher Materials

READ 180 includes a teaching system that provides a clear instructional path for Whole- and Small-Group Instruction, integrated professional development, and resources for assessing students and differentiating instruction.

Teacher Bookshelf
- Core instructional materials
- Resources for differentiating instruction
- Assessment tools
- Professional development support
- Installation software and guides

Resources for Differentiated Instruction
- Book 1: Reading Skills and Strategies
- Book 2: Writing & Grammar Strategies
- Book 3: Strategies for English-Language Learners

Core Instruction
- A comprehensive *Teacher's Edition* for Whole- and Small-Group Instruction
- Includes explicit, systematic skills support
- Provides support in reading comprehension, vocabulary, writing, and grammar
- Anchor Videos build background and mental models

Professional Development
- Online Course: *Best Practices for Reading Intervention*
- Scholastic Red Teacher Handbook
- *Teacher Implementation Guide*

Assessment
- *Placement, Assessment, and Reporting Guide*
- *Test-Taking Strategies*
- *rSkills Tests*

Student Materials

To engage students, *READ 180* Paperbacks present students with age-appropriate, leveled books they can read with success. *READ 180* Audiobooks help students develop good reading skills and habits. The *READ 180* Software includes motivating videos that emphasize content-area based topics. The **rBooks** provide a clear instructional path to keep students engaged.

Stage A

Stage B

Stage C

rBooks
Read. Write. React.
- Interactive worktexts
- High-interest fiction and nonfiction selections
- Daily instruction in reading comprehension, vocabulary, writing, and grammar

Individualized Instructional Software
- Topic Software CDs
- High-interest video segments for building background
- Customized reading instruction and practice

Paperbacks for Independent Reading
- A rich library of fiction and nonfiction
- Carefully leveled books
- Relevant, age-appropriate topics

Audiobooks for Modeled Reading
- Age-appropriate, authentic books on CD
- Provides access to grade level literature
- Includes Reading Coach who models good reading strategies

Targeted Skills Instruction

READ 180 uses age-appropriate materials to teach the skills and knowledge needed to accelerate instruction and bring students to grade level.

Three Stages of Instruction and Support

READ 180 Level	Stage A Elementary	Stage B Middle School	Stage C High School
Level 1	1.5 to 2.5*	1.5 to 2.5	1.5 to 2.5
Level 2	2.5 to 4.0	2.5 to 4.0	2.5 to 4.0
Level 3	4.0 to 6.9	4.0 to 6.0	4.0 to 6.0
Level 4		6.0 to 8.9	6.0 to 12.0

*Denotes reading level

PHONEMIC AWARENESS	A	B	C
Auditory discrimination	✓	✓	✓
Oral blending	✓	✓	✓
Oral segmentation	✓	✓	✓
Phonemic addition and deletion	✓	✓	✓
Phonemic substitution	✓	✓	✓
DECODING, PHONICS, AND SYLLABICATION			
Phonics Skills			
Build automaticity	✓	✓	✓
Connect sound-spellings	✓	✓	✓
Generalize sound-spellings	✓	✓	✓
Decode and pronounce syllables and words	✓	✓	✓
Read sight words and high-frequency words	✓	✓	✓
Build words	✓	✓	✓
Write from dictation	✓	✓	✓
Phonic Elements			
Short vowels	✓	✓	✓
Blends (s-, l-, r-, 3-letter)	✓	✓	✓
Final *e* (*a-e, e-e, i-e, o-e, u-e*)	✓	✓	✓
Digraphs *ch, sh, th, wh, tch*	✓	✓	✓
Vowel /ā/ *ai, ay, eigh, ey, ea*	✓	✓	✓
Vowel /ē/ *ea, ee, e, y, ey*	✓	✓	✓
Vowel /ō/ *o, oa, ow*	✓	✓	✓
Vowel /ī/ *i, igh, y, ieh*	✓	✓	✓
r-controlled vowel /âr/ *air, are, ear, ere, eir*	✓	✓	✓
r-controlled vowel /ôr/ *or, ore, oor, our*	✓	✓	✓
r-controlled vowel /ûr/ *er, ir, ur*	✓	✓	✓
r-controlled vowel /är/ *ar*	✓	✓	✓
Words with /o͞o/ *oo, ue, ew, ough, ou*	✓	✓	✓

DECODING, PHONICS, AND SYLLABICATION (continued)	A	B	C
Vowel /ô/ *a, au, aw, o*	✓	✓	✓
Vowel /ē/ *ea, ai, a*	✓	✓	✓
Vowel /u/ *a, o, au*	✓	✓	✓
Diphthong /ou/ *ou, ow*	✓	✓	✓
Diphthong /oi/ *oi, oy*	✓	✓	✓
Words with /o͞o/ *oo, u, ou*	✓	✓	✓
Words with /ə/ *a, e, i, o, u*	✓	✓	✓
Consonant /f/ *ph, gh*	✓	✓	✓
Consonants /s/ *c*; /j/ *g, dge*	✓	✓	✓
Silent letters *kn, wr, gn, mb*	✓	✓	✓
Syllabication			
Closed syllables	✓	✓	✓
Open syllables	✓	✓	✓
Inflectional endings	✓	✓	✓
Consonant + *-le, -al, -el*	✓	✓	✓
Silent *e* (VC*e*)	✓	✓	✓
r-controlled vowels	✓	✓	✓
Vowel teams	✓	✓	✓
Affixes	✓	✓	✓
Multisyllabic words	✓	✓	✓
Syllable with schwa	✓	✓	✓
FLUENCY			
Build automaticity	✓	✓	✓
Self-assess	✓	✓	✓
Hear modeled fluent reading	✓	✓	✓
Echo reading	✓	✓	✓
Choral reading	✓	✓	✓

<table>
<tr><td rowspan="2">FLUENCY (continued)</td><td colspan="3">READ 180 STAGE</td></tr>
<tr><td>A</td><td>B</td><td>C</td></tr>
<tr><td>Speed drills</td><td>✓</td><td>✓</td><td>✓</td></tr>
<tr><td>Read with prosody</td><td>✓</td><td>✓</td><td>✓</td></tr>
<tr><td>Self-correct</td><td>✓</td><td>✓</td><td>✓</td></tr>
<tr><td>Repeated-timed reading</td><td>✓</td><td>✓</td><td>✓</td></tr>
<tr><td>Read with expression</td><td>✓</td><td>✓</td><td>✓</td></tr>
<tr><td>Adjust reading rate</td><td>✓</td><td>✓</td><td>✓</td></tr>
<tr><td>Use natural/consistent pace</td><td>✓</td><td>✓</td><td>✓</td></tr>
<tr><td>Use correct phrasing</td><td>✓</td><td>✓</td><td>✓</td></tr>
<tr><td>Read phrase-cued text</td><td>✓</td><td>✓</td><td>✓</td></tr>
<tr><td>Oral recitation</td><td>✓</td><td>✓</td><td>✓</td></tr>
<tr><td>Readers theater</td><td>✓</td><td>✓</td><td>✓</td></tr>
<tr><td colspan="4">SPELLING</td></tr>
<tr><td>Recognize sound-spelling patterns</td><td>✓</td><td>✓</td><td>✓</td></tr>
<tr><td>Use spelling rules</td><td>✓</td><td>✓</td><td>✓</td></tr>
<tr><td>Build words</td><td>✓</td><td>✓</td><td>✓</td></tr>
<tr><td>Sort words by pattern</td><td>✓</td><td>✓</td><td>✓</td></tr>
<tr><td>Correct common errors</td><td>✓</td><td>✓</td><td>✓</td></tr>
<tr><td>Spell from dictation</td><td>✓</td><td>✓</td><td>✓</td></tr>
<tr><td>Proofread</td><td>✓</td><td>✓</td><td>✓</td></tr>
<tr><td colspan="4">VOCABULARY AND WORD STUDY</td></tr>
<tr><td>Word families</td><td>✓</td><td>✓</td><td>✓</td></tr>
<tr><td>Compound words</td><td>✓</td><td>✓</td><td>✓</td></tr>
<tr><td>Context clues</td><td>✓</td><td>✓</td><td>✓</td></tr>
<tr><td>Multiple-meaning words</td><td>✓</td><td>✓</td><td>✓</td></tr>
<tr><td>Homophones</td><td>✓</td><td>✓</td><td>✓</td></tr>
<tr><td>Homographs</td><td>✓</td><td>✓</td><td>✓</td></tr>
<tr><td>Use a dictionary</td><td>✓</td><td>✓</td><td>✓</td></tr>
<tr><td>Synonyms</td><td>✓</td><td>✓</td><td>✓</td></tr>
<tr><td>Antonyms</td><td>✓</td><td>✓</td><td>✓</td></tr>
<tr><td>Denotation and connotation</td><td>✓</td><td>✓</td><td>✓</td></tr>
<tr><td>Use a thesaurus</td><td>✓</td><td>✓</td><td>✓</td></tr>
<tr><td>Prefixes</td><td>✓</td><td>✓</td><td>✓</td></tr>
<tr><td>Suffixes</td><td>✓</td><td>✓</td><td>✓</td></tr>
<tr><td>Noun endings</td><td>✓</td><td>✓</td><td>✓</td></tr>
<tr><td>Verb endings</td><td>✓</td><td>✓</td><td>✓</td></tr>
<tr><td>Inflectional endings with and without base change</td><td>✓</td><td>✓</td><td>✓</td></tr>
<tr><td>Contractions</td><td>✓</td><td>✓</td><td>✓</td></tr>
<tr><td>Greek and Latin roots</td><td>✓</td><td>✓</td><td>✓</td></tr>
<tr><td>Words origins</td><td>✓</td><td>✓</td><td>✓</td></tr>
<tr><td>Idioms</td><td>✓</td><td>✓</td><td>✓</td></tr>
<tr><td>Similes and metaphors</td><td>✓</td><td>✓</td><td>✓</td></tr>
<tr><td>Figurative language</td><td>✓</td><td>✓</td><td>✓</td></tr>
</table>

<table>
<tr><td rowspan="2">COMPREHENSION AND CRITICAL THINKING</td><td colspan="3">READ 180 STAGE</td></tr>
<tr><td>A</td><td>B</td><td>C</td></tr>
<tr><td colspan="4">Purposes for Reading</td></tr>
<tr><td>Reading for enjoyment</td><td>✓</td><td>✓</td><td>✓</td></tr>
<tr><td>Read for information and to answer questions</td><td>✓</td><td>✓</td><td>✓</td></tr>
<tr><td>Read independently and with others</td><td>✓</td><td>✓</td><td>✓</td></tr>
<tr><td>Set and follow purpose for reading</td><td>✓</td><td>✓</td><td>✓</td></tr>
<tr><td>Self-select reading materials</td><td>✓</td><td>✓</td><td>✓</td></tr>
<tr><td colspan="4">Reading Behaviors</td></tr>
<tr><td>Use graphic organizers to represent text information</td><td>✓</td><td>✓</td><td>✓</td></tr>
<tr><td>Use self-monitoring strategies (metacognition)</td><td>✓</td><td>✓</td><td>✓</td></tr>
<tr><td>Visualize</td><td>✓</td><td>✓</td><td>✓</td></tr>
<tr><td>Ask and answer questions about text</td><td>✓</td><td>✓</td><td>✓</td></tr>
<tr><td>Read independent and instructional-level materials</td><td>✓</td><td>✓</td><td>✓</td></tr>
<tr><td>Use prereading strategies</td><td>✓</td><td>✓</td><td>✓</td></tr>
<tr><td>Use prior knowledge to comprehend texts</td><td>✓</td><td>✓</td><td>✓</td></tr>
<tr><td>Read across texts</td><td>✓</td><td>✓</td><td>✓</td></tr>
<tr><td>Connect ideas and themes across texts</td><td>✓</td><td>✓</td><td>✓</td></tr>
<tr><td>Relate literary works to historical context</td><td>✓</td><td>✓</td><td>✓</td></tr>
<tr><td>Relate texts to personal experience</td><td>✓</td><td>✓</td><td>✓</td></tr>
<tr><td colspan="4">Software and rBook Skills</td></tr>
<tr><td>Read for detail</td><td>✓</td><td>✓</td><td>✓</td></tr>
<tr><td>Sequence of events</td><td>✓</td><td>✓</td><td>✓</td></tr>
<tr><td>Main idea and details</td><td>✓</td><td>✓</td><td>✓</td></tr>
<tr><td>Summarize</td><td>✓</td><td>✓</td><td>✓</td></tr>
<tr><td>Cause and effect</td><td>✓</td><td>✓</td><td>✓</td></tr>
<tr><td>Compare and contrast</td><td>✓</td><td>✓</td><td>✓</td></tr>
<tr><td>Problem and solution</td><td>✓</td><td>✓</td><td>✓</td></tr>
<tr><td>Make inferences</td><td>✓</td><td>✓</td><td>✓</td></tr>
<tr><td>Draw conclusions</td><td>✓</td><td>✓</td><td>✓</td></tr>
<tr><td>Story elements</td><td>✓</td><td>✓</td><td>✓</td></tr>
<tr><td colspan="4">Supplementary Skills</td></tr>
<tr><td>Distinguish important/unimportant details</td><td>✓</td><td></td><td></td></tr>
<tr><td>Make predictions</td><td>✓</td><td>✓</td><td>✓</td></tr>
<tr><td>Identify point of view</td><td>✓</td><td>✓</td><td>✓</td></tr>
<tr><td>Identify author's purpose</td><td>✓</td><td>✓</td><td>✓</td></tr>
<tr><td>Distinguish fact and opinion</td><td>✓</td><td>✓</td><td>✓</td></tr>
<tr><td>Make judgments</td><td>✓</td><td>✓</td><td>✓</td></tr>
<tr><td>Identify bias</td><td>✓</td><td></td><td></td></tr>
<tr><td>Identify persuasion and propaganda</td><td></td><td>✓</td><td>✓</td></tr>
<tr><td>Evaluate sources and evidence</td><td></td><td>✓</td><td>✓</td></tr>
<tr><td>Evaluate author's viewpoint</td><td></td><td>✓</td><td>✓</td></tr>
</table>

Left table

COMPREHENSION AND CRITICAL THINKING (continued)	A	B	C
Evaluate author's purpose			✓
Support judgments			✓
Support generalizations			✓
Evaluate literary merit			✓
Study Skills			
Skim and scan	✓	✓	✓
Take notes	✓	✓	✓
Mark up texts	✓	✓	✓
Use multiple sources			✓
TEXT FEATURES (See also Genre: Functional Text)			
Bar graphs	✓	✓	✓
Bold and italic type	✓	✓	✓
Captions and labels	✓	✓	✓
Charts	✓	✓	✓
Diagrams	✓	✓	✓
Flowcharts		✓	
Labels	✓	✓	✓
Line graphs and pie/circle graphs	✓	✓	✓
Maps and floor plans	✓	✓	✓
Photos and illustrations	✓	✓	✓
Schedules	✓	✓	
Time lines		✓	✓
Titles and subheadings	✓	✓	✓
Literary Skills			
Analyze character	✓	✓	✓
Analyze setting	✓	✓	✓
Analyze plot	✓	✓	✓
Analyze theme	✓	✓	✓
Universal theme			✓
Mood	✓	✓	✓
Tone	✓	✓	✓
Conflict	✓	✓	✓
Flashback	✓	✓	✓
Imagery	✓	✓	✓
Simile and metaphor	✓	✓	✓
Suspense	✓	✓	✓
Symbolism	✓	✓	✓
Dialogue	✓	✓	✓
Foreshadowing		✓	✓
Irony		✓	✓
Parody			✓
Rhyme and repetition	✓	✓	✓

Right table

COMPREHENSION AND CRITICAL THINKING (continued)	A	B	C
Rhyme scheme			✓
Onomatopoeia	✓	✓	
Hyperbole	✓		
Personification	✓		
Alliteration	✓	✓	
Assonance	✓	✓	
Poetic devices/elements	✓	✓	✓
Soliloquy			✓
Sonnet			✓
GENRE/TEXT STRUCTURE			
Culture			
Read and respond to texts from diverse cultures	✓	✓	✓
Analyze how literary works reflect the culture of the author	✓	✓	✓
Fiction, Nonfiction, Poetry, and Drama			
Adventure, crime, and suspense	✓	✓	✓
Autobiography	✓	✓	✓
Biography	✓	✓	✓
Classic	✓	✓	✓
Content-area text	✓	✓	✓
Debate/opinion	✓	✓	✓
Drama/play	✓	✓	✓
Editorial	✓	✓	✓
Encyclopedia entry	✓	✓	✓
Fable/Myth/Folktale	✓	✓	✓
Fantasy	✓	✓	✓
Fiction	✓	✓	✓
Graphic classic	✓	✓	✓
Historical documents	✓	✓	✓
Historical fiction	✓	✓	✓
Horror		✓	✓
Humor	✓	✓	✓
Letters/diaries	✓	✓	✓
Magazine and news articles	✓	✓	✓
Memoir	✓	✓	✓
Mystery	✓	✓	✓
Nonfiction	✓	✓	✓
Parody			✓
Personal narrative	✓	✓	✓
Poetry	✓	✓	✓
Profile	✓	✓	✓

GENRE/TEXT STRUCTURE (continued)	A	B	C
Realistic fiction	✓	✓	✓
Science fiction	✓	✓	✓
Short story	✓	✓	✓
Soliloquy			✓
Functional Text *(See also Comprehension: Text Features)*			
Advertisement		✓	✓
Book review	✓	✓	✓
Budget			✓
Editorial cartoon			✓
Electronic text/Web site	✓	✓	✓
Forms and applications		✓	✓
Instructions	✓	✓	✓
Packaging/covers/labels	✓	✓	✓
Posters and signs	✓	✓	
Sales receipt			✓
Schedule	✓	✓	
LITERARY RESPONSE			
Explain likes and dislikes related to a reading selection	✓	✓	✓
Relate texts to social issues	✓	✓	✓
Respond to texts through discussion	✓	✓	✓
Respond to texts through writing	✓	✓	✓
Support responses to texts by referring to relevant aspects of text and own experience	✓	✓	✓
WRITING			
rBook **Writing Types**			
Descriptive	✓	✓	✓
Expository	✓	✓	✓
Expository summary	✓	✓	✓
Literature response	✓	✓	✓
Literature review	✓	✓	
Literature critique			✓
Narrative	✓	✓	✓
Persuasive	✓	✓	✓
Supplementary Assignment Types			
Fictional narrative	✓	✓	✓
Personal narrative	✓	✓	✓
Realistic narrative	✓	✓	✓
Fantasy	✓	✓	✓
Biographical narrative	✓	✓	✓
Historical narrative			✓
Narrative composition/essay	✓	✓	✓
Description of a person	✓	✓	✓

WRITING (continued)	A	B	C
Description of a setting	✓	✓	✓
Compare and contrast	✓	✓	✓
Character sketch	✓	✓	✓
Descriptive composition/essay	✓	✓	✓
Cause and effect	✓	✓	✓
Content-area/social studies report	✓	✓	✓
Book synopsis	✓	✓	✓
News article	✓	✓	✓
Informative article/essay	✓	✓	✓
Nonfiction summary	✓	✓	✓
Expository composition/essay	✓	✓	✓
Opinion	✓	✓	✓
Review	✓	✓	✓
Persuasive speech	✓	✓	✓
Persuasive composition/essay	✓	✓	✓
Poetry	✓	✓	✓
Letters and notes	✓	✓	✓
How-to paragraph	✓	✓	✓
Business letter	✓	✓	✓
Announcement	✓	✓	✓
Résumé		✓	✓
Reflective essay			✓
Writer's Craft/Skills			
Character details	✓	✓	✓
Combine sentences	✓	✓	✓
Defend an opinion		✓	
Formal and informal language	✓	✓	✓
Interesting beginnings	✓	✓	✓
Organize details	✓	✓	✓
Paragraph building	✓	✓	✓
Sequence words	✓	✓	✓
Specific words	✓	✓	✓
Summarize	✓	✓	✓
Supporting reasons	✓	✓	✓
Synonyms	✓	✓	✓
Topic sentence	✓	✓	✓
Transition words	✓	✓	✓
Use dialogue	✓	✓	✓
Use figurative language	✓	✓	✓
Use four types of sentences	✓	✓	✓
Use metaphors and similes	✓	✓	✓
Write conclusions	✓	✓	✓
Writing in first and third person	✓	✓	✓

WRITING (continued)	READ 180 STAGE A	B	C
Research Skills			
Bibliography	✓	✓	✓
Choose and narrow a topic	✓	✓	✓
Find and record information	✓	✓	✓
Identify features of a research report	✓	✓	✓
Locate and use sources	✓	✓	✓
Organize information	✓	✓	✓
Outline	✓	✓	✓
Take notes	✓	✓	✓
Use electronic sources	✓	✓	✓
GRAMMAR, USAGE, AND MECHANICS			
Identify sentences and fragments	✓	✓	✓
Sentence types	✓	✓	✓
Subject and predicate	✓	✓	✓
Dependent and independent clauses	✓	✓	✓
Correct word order	✓	✓	✓
Common and proper nouns	✓	✓	✓
Singular and plural nouns	✓	✓	✓
Action verbs	✓	✓	✓
Present-tense verbs	✓	✓	✓
Past-tense verbs	✓	✓	✓
Main and helping verbs	✓	✓	✓
Future-tense verbs	✓	✓	✓
Irregular verbs	✓	✓	✓
Subject-verb agreement	✓	✓	✓
Subject and object pronouns	✓	✓	✓
Possessive nouns	✓	✓	✓
Adjectives	✓	✓	✓
Adjectives that compare	✓	✓	✓
Adverbs	✓	✓	✓
Adverbs that compare	✓	✓	✓
Contractions	✓	✓	✓
Avoiding double-negatives	✓	✓	✓
Correct sentence fragments	✓	✓	✓
Compound sentences	✓	✓	✓
Correct run-on sentences	✓	✓	✓
Combine sentences with phrases	✓	✓	✓
Past-perfect tense	✓	✓	✓
Capitalization	✓	✓	✓
Commas	✓	✓	✓
End punctuation	✓	✓	✓
Quotation marks	✓	✓	✓

ENGLISH-LANGUAGE LEARNERS	READ 180 STAGE A	B	C
Language-Development			
Use academic language	✓	✓	✓
Use culturally appropriate language	✓	✓	✓
Use formal and informal language	✓	✓	✓
Use social language	✓	✓	✓
Vocabulary Contexts (Oral Language)			
Classroom	✓	✓	✓
Community	✓	✓	✓
Mathematics/numbers	✓	✓	✓
News/media	✓	✓	✓
Social occasions and vacations	✓	✓	✓
Ask questions	✓	✓	✓
Calendar and time expressions	✓	✓	✓
Idiomatic language	✓	✓	✓
Commands/requests	✓	✓	✓
Computer terms	✓	✓	✓
Ask and give directions	✓	✓	✓
Interviewing	✓	✓	✓
Introductions and greetings	✓	✓	✓
Parts of books	✓	✓	✓
Special occasions	✓	✓	✓
Telephone conversations	✓	✓	✓
Weather terms	✓	✓	✓
Inflection			
Emphasizing syllables and words	✓	✓	✓
Inflection and meaning	✓	✓	✓
Pronunciation and inflection	✓	✓	✓
Rhythms and rhyme	✓	✓	✓
Sounds of English			
Distinguish sounds	✓	✓	✓
Easily confused words	✓	✓	✓
Word Study (See also Grammar)			
Phrasal verbs	✓	✓	✓
Count and non-count nouns	✓	✓	✓
TEST-TAKING STRATEGIES			
Reading Test Skills			
Answer fill-in-the blanks	✓	✓	✓
Answer proofreading questions	✓	✓	✓
Identify literal and interpretive questions	✓	✓	✓
Justify and check answer	✓	✓	✓
Make an educated guess	✓	✓	✓
Preview questions	✓	✓	✓

	READ 180 STAGE		
TEST-TAKING STRATEGIES (continued)	**A**	**B**	**C**
Restate the question	✓	✓	✓
Use cue words to understand questions	✓	✓	✓
Use text evidence	✓	✓	✓
Use vocabulary strategies	✓	✓	✓
Open-ended questions	✓	✓	✓
Use test time effectively	✓	✓	✓
Writing Test Skills			
Analyze writing prompts	✓	✓	✓
Identify narrative writing prompts	✓	✓	✓
Identify expository writing prompts	✓	✓	✓
Identify persuasive writing prompts	✓	✓	✓
Restate the prompt	✓	✓	✓
Generate thoughts	✓	✓	✓
Create an outline	✓	✓	✓
Understand evaluation criteria	✓	✓	✓
CAREERS			
Explore career choices in varied fields	✓	✓	✓
Identify literacy and other skills used in varied careers	✓	✓	✓
Read workplace documents	✓	✓	✓
Identify education required for varied careers	✓	✓	✓
LISTENING, SPEAKING, AND VIEWING			
Listen for a variety of purposes	✓	✓	✓
Use strategies for active listening	✓	✓	✓
Evaluate speaker's message	✓	✓	✓
Listen to fluent reading models	✓	✓	✓
Speak for different purposes and audiences	✓	✓	✓
Use academic language orally	✓	✓	✓
Speak to share information and views	✓	✓	✓
Support spoken messages with evidence and reasons	✓	✓	✓
Use strategies for active viewing	✓	✓	✓
View and interpret messages of visual media	✓	✓	✓
View varied media for a variety of purposes	✓	✓	✓

"There has been success in all areas. I would say spelling, comprehension, and fluency were areas of great improvement for all the kids."
—Carrie Roberts, *READ 180* Teacher

Differentiated Instruction

Differentiated learning is considering what students know and adapting teaching methods, using leveled materials, and adjusting the amount and pacing of instruction to meet each student's needs. Not all struggling readers have difficulty with the same aspects of reading.

The *READ 180* Topic Software automatically assesses and provides individualized support, skills practice, and feedback to students based on their specific needs in reading, word recognition, and spelling.

• Ongoing data collection allows the Software to adjust instruction according to student's learning needs.

• Students get intensive, differentiated skills practice and instruction.

• Students receive immediate, corrective feedback based on their specific errors.

• Customized reading and spelling activities target students' needs based on initial assessments and prior activities.

• Software settings allow students to vary the reading pace, hear decoding tips for words, and receive support in five languages.

• Students can choose to go back and watch the video or reread the passage when they need more support.

Learning Zones

The next pages provide a screen-by-screen overview of the four Learning Zones of the *READ 180* Topic Software.

Reading Zone
Students view a video and read a leveled passage. Phonics, fluency, vocabulary, and comprehension skills instruction are grounded in practice and application.

Word Zone
Students master words from the reading passage as they practice decoding and rapid word recognition.

Spelling Zone
Student responses on an initial assessment generate a customized word list for spelling mastery. Activities present varied opportunities for practice, including proofreading.

Success Zone
Students practice and apply comprehension skills as they continue to build fluency. They demonstrate success through a final oral recording of their passage. Upon completing this zone, students move on to a new segment.

> "*READ 180* has boosted my students' confidence academically and emotionally. Students love checking their progress on the Software. It reinforces the fact that they can be successful at reading."—Allie Nixon, *READ 180* Teacher

The **Reading Zone** is where scaffolded instruction begins. Phonics, fluency, vocabulary, and comprehension are the key skills developed and practiced.

Video

Students will...

- Watch a motivating video to gain background information and develop a mental model.
- Have the option to hear a summary in Spanish, Cantonese, Haitian Creole, Hmong, or Vietnamese before viewing.

Snake Stalker video

TEACHER CHECK-IN Have students read the passage aloud to assess fluency.

Passage

Students will...

- Repeatedly read one of four leveled passages with varying degrees of computer support.
- Read along with computer audio at student-selected speeds, either one word at a time or phrase by phrase.
- Use the Practice button to highlight text for reading practice at various speeds without audio support.
- Make an initial audio recording of the passage and self-assess fluency.
- Learn targeted vocabulary.

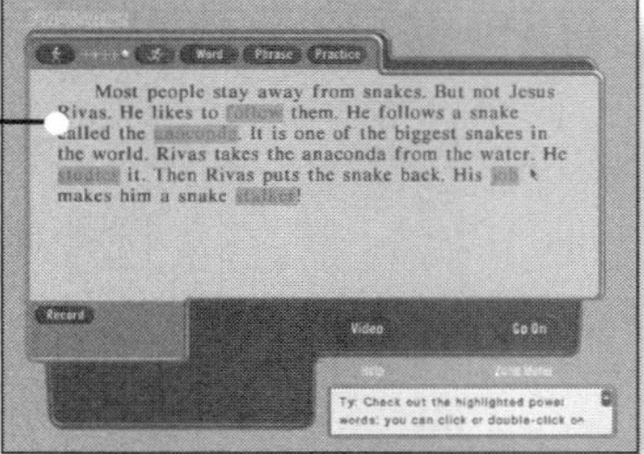

Level 1

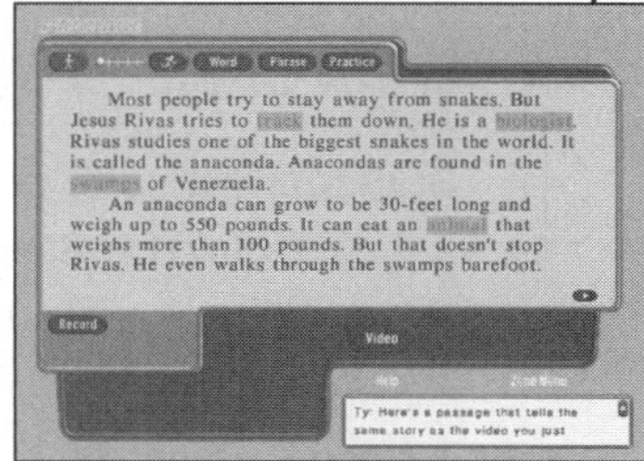

Level 2

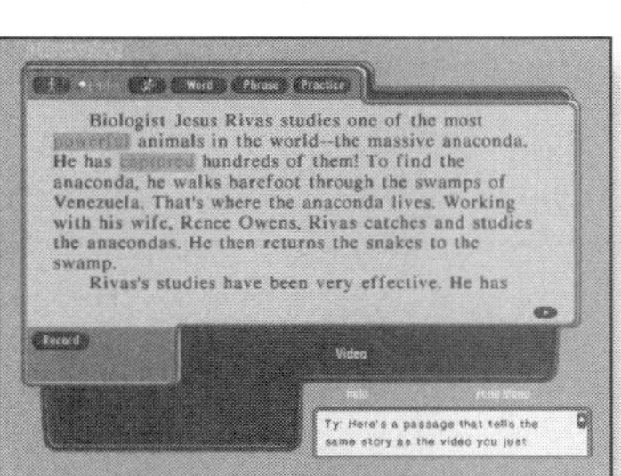

Level 3

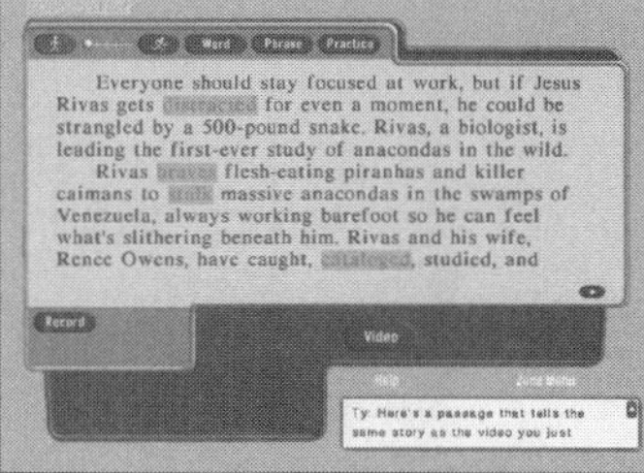

Level 4

Quick Check

Students will...

- Answer multiple-choice questions as a vocabulary and comprehension check.
- Receive immediate feedback about their answers.
- Be scored based on first attempt.

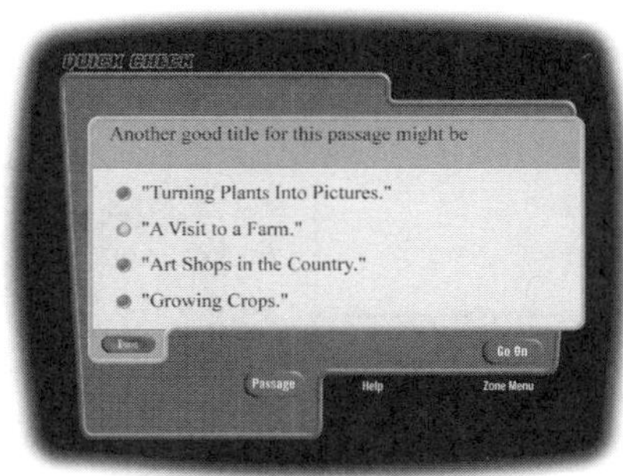

READING ZONE MASTERY
To complete the Reading Zone for each segment, students must correctly answer ten comprehension and vocabulary questions.

In the **Word Zone**, students receive systematic instruction in decoding and word recognition as they build automaticity. The instruction takes place through supportive, engaging activities.

Word Assessment

Students will...

- Hear words from the passage and identify them in a list.
- Find out which words they did not identify quickly or accurately. These become their Study Words.

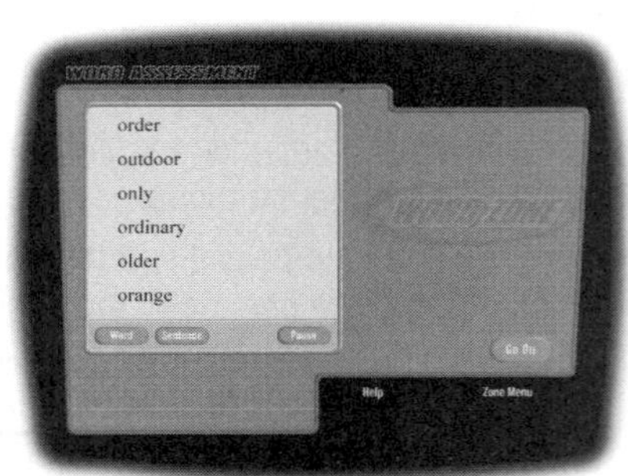

> **TEACHER CHECK-IN** Ask students to read their Study Words. Listen as they record Study Words.

Word Clinic

Students will...

- Be introduced to Study Words.
- See and hear concrete tips on how to decode their Study Words.
- Make an audio recording of Study Words.

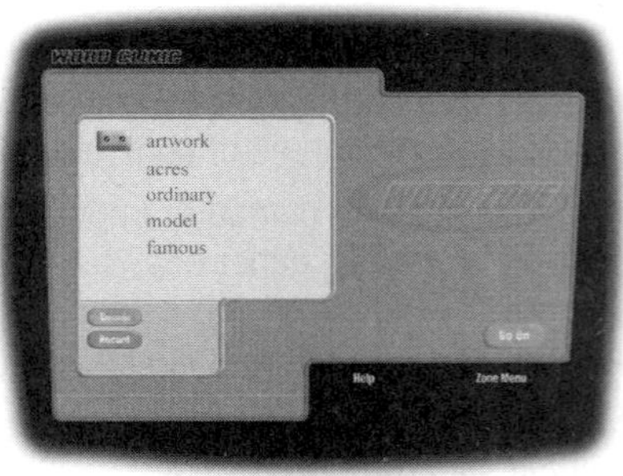

Word Match

Students will...

- Review previously studied words to maintain mastery.
- Hear personal recordings of individual Study or Review Words and match the recordings to written words.

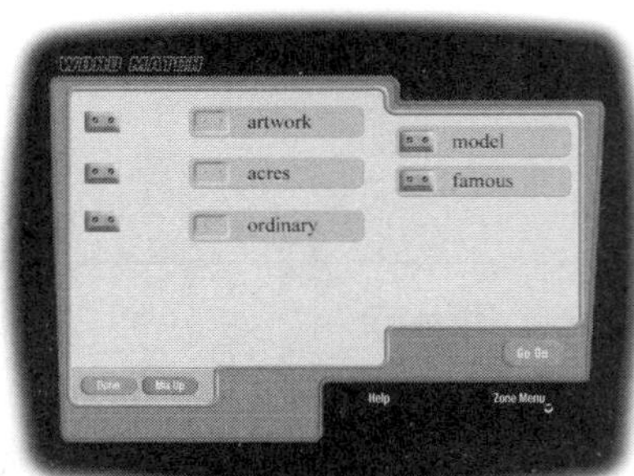

> *ZONE MASTERY*
> *Before exiting each Zone, students receive on-screen summaries detailing their progress.*

Self Check

Students will...

- Compare their recordings with an announcer's reading of each Study or Review Word.
- Assess their own accuracy by clicking thumbs up or thumbs down.

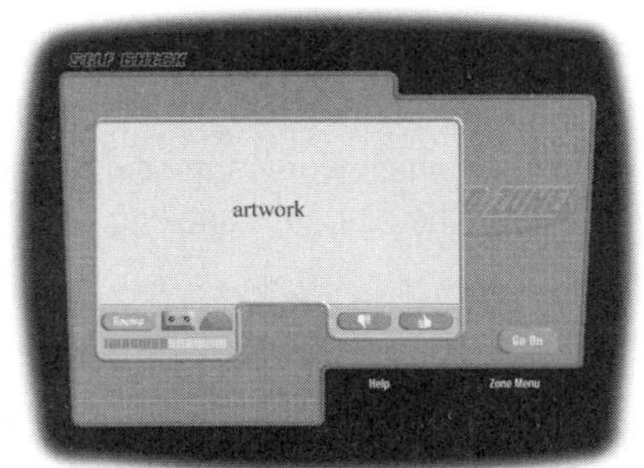

Speed Challenge

Students will...

- Practice rapid word identification.
- Hear a Study or Review Word and select it from a list quickly.

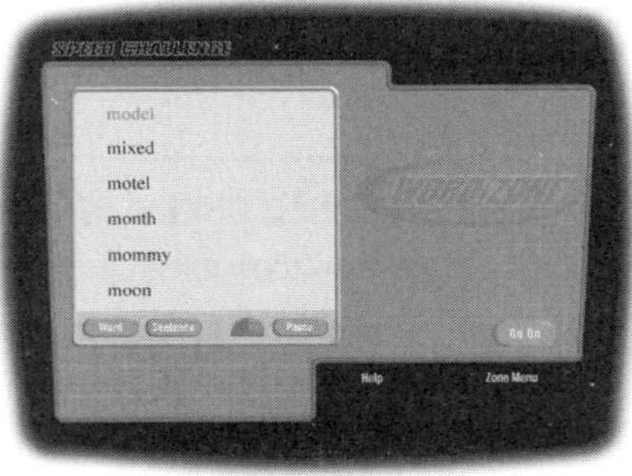

Review

Students will...

- Review words that still need to be practiced.
- Hear each Review Word and select it quickly from a list.

This activity is triggered only when data indicates that the student needs further practice.

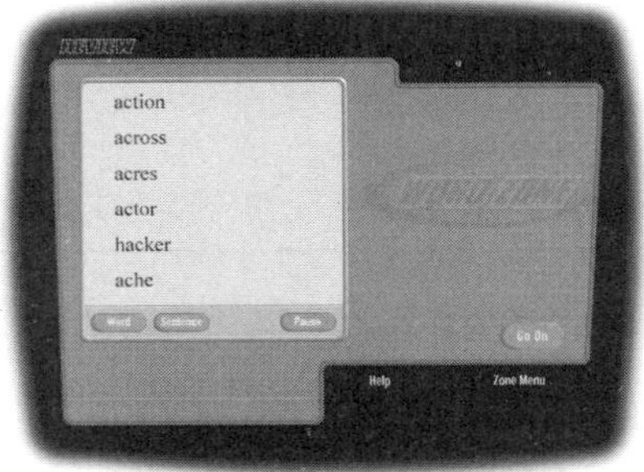

WORD ZONE MASTERY
Word Zone work is complete for a segment when the student has demonstrated mastery and fluency of all the Target Words from the passage. Before exiting each zone, students receive on-screen summary reports detailing their progress so far.

In the **Spelling Zone**, students practice spelling and receive immediate corrective feedback.

Spelling Assessment

Students will...

- Hear and spell words from the passage.
- Find out which words they did not spell correctly. These become the student's spelling Study Words.

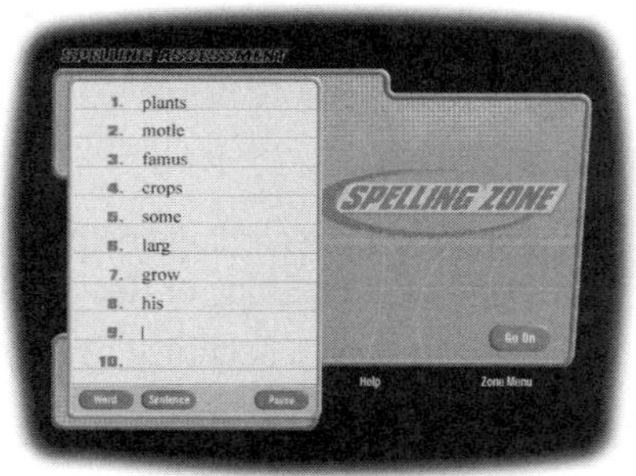

Spelling Clinic

Students will...

- Be introduced to Study Words.
- Spell each Study Word.

TEACHER CHECK-IN Ask students to read their spelling Study Words.

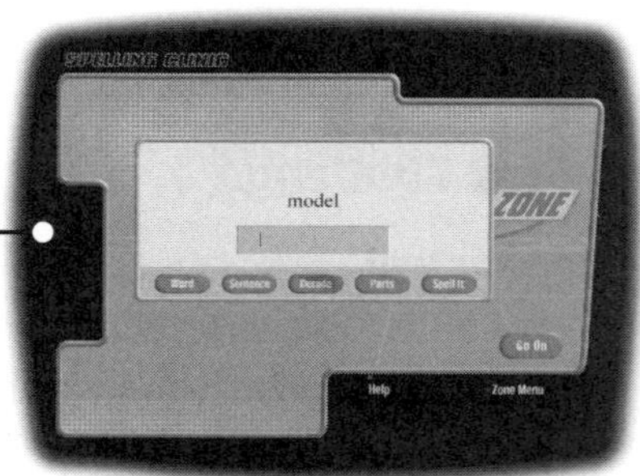

Spelling Challenge

Students will...

- Hear a word and spell it quickly.
- Review previously studied words.

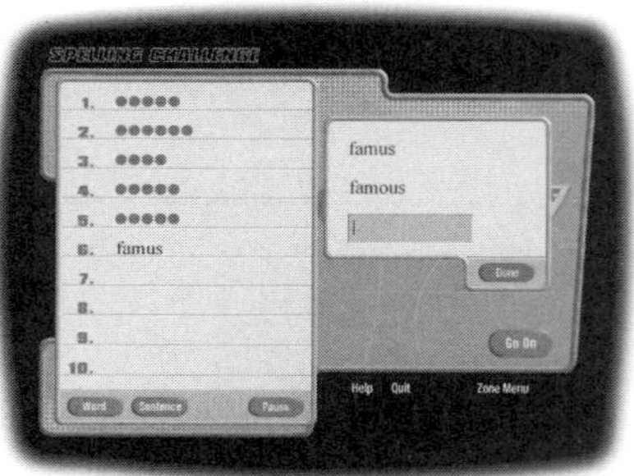

Proofreading

Students will...

- Proofread sentences with misspellings.
- Identify misspelled words and choose the correct spellings from a list.
- Receive immediate feedback about their answers.

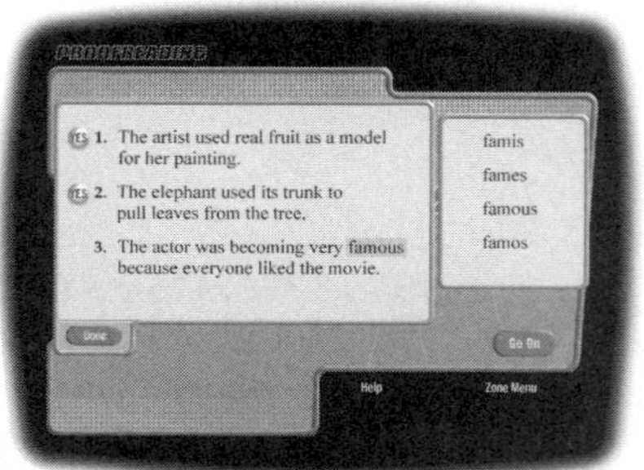

SPELLING ZONE MASTERY
To complete the Spelling Zone for each segment, students must correctly spell a minimum of 6 to 12 new Study Words, depending on their level.

Students reach the **Success Zone** only after they have achieved all the requirements of the other zones and have demonstrated mastery of all words in the passage. In the Success Zone, comprehension becomes the main focus. Oral reading fluency is demonstrated in a final recording.

Discrepancy Passages

Students will...

- Apply comprehension strategies to compare modified versions of the passage.
- Choose the version that accurately summarizes the original passage.

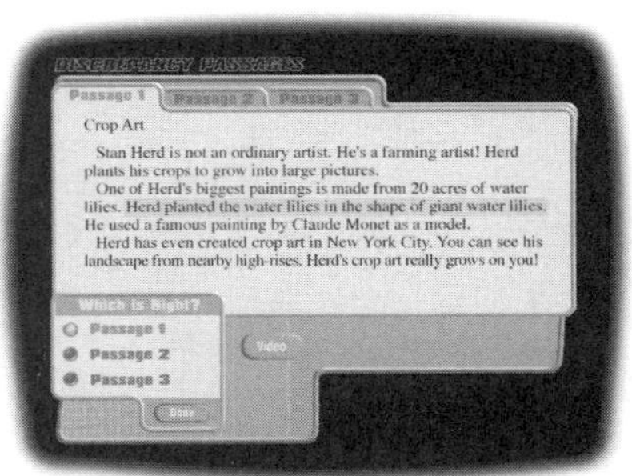

Context Passages

Students will...

- Read passages and select words that will accurately fill in the blanks.
- Apply comprehension and vocabulary strategies to determine the correct word.

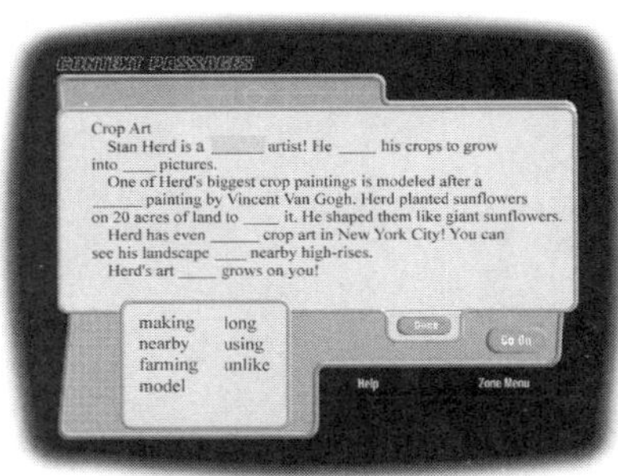

Final Recording

TEACHER CHECK-IN Listen to students read the passage aloud to assess fluency.

Students will...

- Make an audio recording of the passage to demonstrate mastery and share success.
- Assess their recording with a timed fluency self-check.

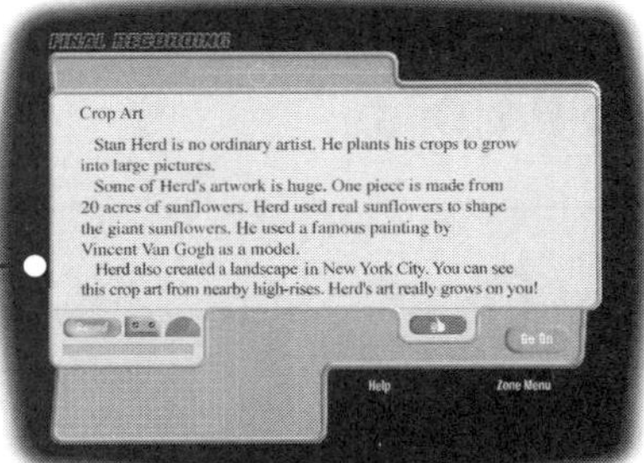

SUCCESS ZONE MASTERY
After students make a final recording of their passage and listen to this recording, they move on to a new segment.

Topic Software Content

The *READ 180* Software includes motivating videos that emphasize content-area topics. Each is designed to motivate students and build background for reading. Below are the Topic Software CD selections for Stage B.

PEOPLE & CULTURES

Art Attack

Video segments convey the value and variety of artistic expression.

The art world is made up of diverse people with unique visions and talent.

Crop Art An unusual artist doesn't paint pictures, he plants them.

Halls of Fame High school students at a performing arts school reach for the stars.

Young at Art A teenager has become "the new Picasso."

STOMP A troupe of dancers has found a unique way to make music.

Help Wanted

Video segments feature accomplished individuals from many backgrounds.

Following our talents and interests can lead to successful careers.

Jump Shot Photographer Bruce Thorson captures sports action with a camera.

In the Funnies Robb Armstrong creates a comic strip based on his life.

Building Dreams Linda Alvarado is breaking ground in the traditionally male fields of construction and baseball.

Blast Off! Dr. Mae Jemison uses courage and teamwork to launch her career as an astronaut.

Beating the Odds

People who have overcome obstacles inspire others.

Feel the Beat Though profoundly deaf, a percussionist uses her other senses to create music.

Second Chance Karen Medville cleared many hurdles to become a scientist.

Little Rock Nine African-American students make history by attending a formerly segregated school.

Write Direction Troubled teens turn their pain into words.

SCIENCE & MATH

Disaster!

Show Me the Money!

Extreme Sports

Survive

Extreme environmental conditions can produce devastating results.

Flood! Massive flooding of the Mississippi wreaks havoc in the Midwest.

Earthquake! Violent rumblings from the earth's core rock the seaside community of Santa Cruz, California.

Avalanche! An avalanche buries a quaint Icelandic village.

Volcano! Volcanic activity on a Caribbean island forces mass evacuation.

People are capable of adapting to extreme environments.

Braving Alaska One family carves a life out of ice in Alaska's frozen tundra.

Out of the Dust An award-winning author conveys the hardships of the Dust Bowl.

In Search of Rain West African nomads forge an existence in the dry desert.

Take a Dive Sailors on a submarine sacrifice many of life's basics.

> **Topic Software sparks engaging discussion.**

You and the Law

The U.S. government has a complex system for manufacturing and protecting hard cash.

Making Money The U.S. Treasury holds the recipe for creating new bills.

Bogus Bills Counterfeiters try to beat the system by printing their own money.

Fighting Forgery The U.S. government fights back to outsmart counterfeiters.

Mangled Money Despite rigorous testing, money still ends up mangled.

Laws and regulations can spark discussion and debate.

Ban the Boards How can cities allow skateboarding and avoid liability?

What Curfew? Should a 16 year old be fined for breaking a city curfew he didn't know existed?

No Passing Should students with poor grades be banned from driver's ed?

Taking Mom to the Mall Should kids be forced to bring an adult to the mall?

The Whole World Watched

Some sports require a combination of adrenaline, skill, and an understanding of science.

Extreme Snowboarding Knowing their equipment helps snowboarders conquer the slopes.

Extreme Biking Mountain bikers take on tough terrain.

Extreme Kayaking Kayakers navigate the world's fiercest river.

Extreme Surfing Skyboarders surf the air while falling at 120 mph.

Some events capture the attention of the entire world.

A Dark Day in Dallas America's beloved 35th President is assassinated.

One Giant Leap America wins the space race when Neil Armstrong walks on the moon.

Freedom in South Africa Nelson Mandela leads the fight to end apartheid.

The People's Princess The world mourns the sudden death of Lady Diana Spencer.

> **Topic Software promotes awareness of newsworthy events from the past.**

Data-Driven Instruction

READ 180 Software

READ 180 Software provides differentiated, data-driven instruction. As the program gathers information about the student's abilities, the Software makes immediate instructional decisions based on the most recent data. This constant feedback provides the most detailed form of assessment in the following critical areas.

Phonics and Word Recognition

For initial instructional placement, the Software assesses individual word recognition according to two criteria: accuracy and fluency. Mastery of a word is when a student recognizes it successfully two out of three times (accuracy) in under 1.25 seconds (fluency).

Once instruction is underway, the student must continue to accurately and fluently identify words 85 percent of the time, and maintain that level of word recognition on a continuing basis. Ongoing assessment ensures this high level of mastery is maintained.

Fluency

The Software assesses oral reading performance at regular intervals by capturing an authentic recording of a student reading a text passage. Standards for acceptable oral reading performance can be determined by the teacher for individual students. Oral reading samples are also an excellent tool for students to set goals and assess their own progress.

Spelling

In an initial assessment, students are expected to generate the correct spelling of an individualized set of words. Following instruction, students must correctly spell the words they missed in three consecutive trials, interspersed with review words, as criteria for mastery. Although successful whole-word completion is required for mastery, the correct letter sequence is used as a measure of progress.

Reading and Comprehension

A student's ability to accurately read and comprehend text passages is determined in two ways. First, a student is given three similar passages to read. Mastery is achieved when the student can identify the one that is factually correct. A second form of connected text assessment requires the student to complete a passage by choosing the missing words from a list of choices.

> "*READ 180* is successful because it integrates technology into the classroom. The videos give students a mental image they can draw from."
> —Pam Zamaris, *READ 180* Coordinator

Scholastic Achievement Manager

SAM, the *Scholastic Achievement Manager*, continuously collects student data and organizes it for efficient use. The *READ 180* Instructional Model provides specified time slots for differentiating instruction so that teachers can act on essential data, identify priority areas, and meet goals.

Using data to guide instruction can help teachers:

- Identify priority areas and plan differentiated instruction.
- Set and monitor reading goals with students.
- Place students in groups based on their needs.
- Communicate students' reading progress.

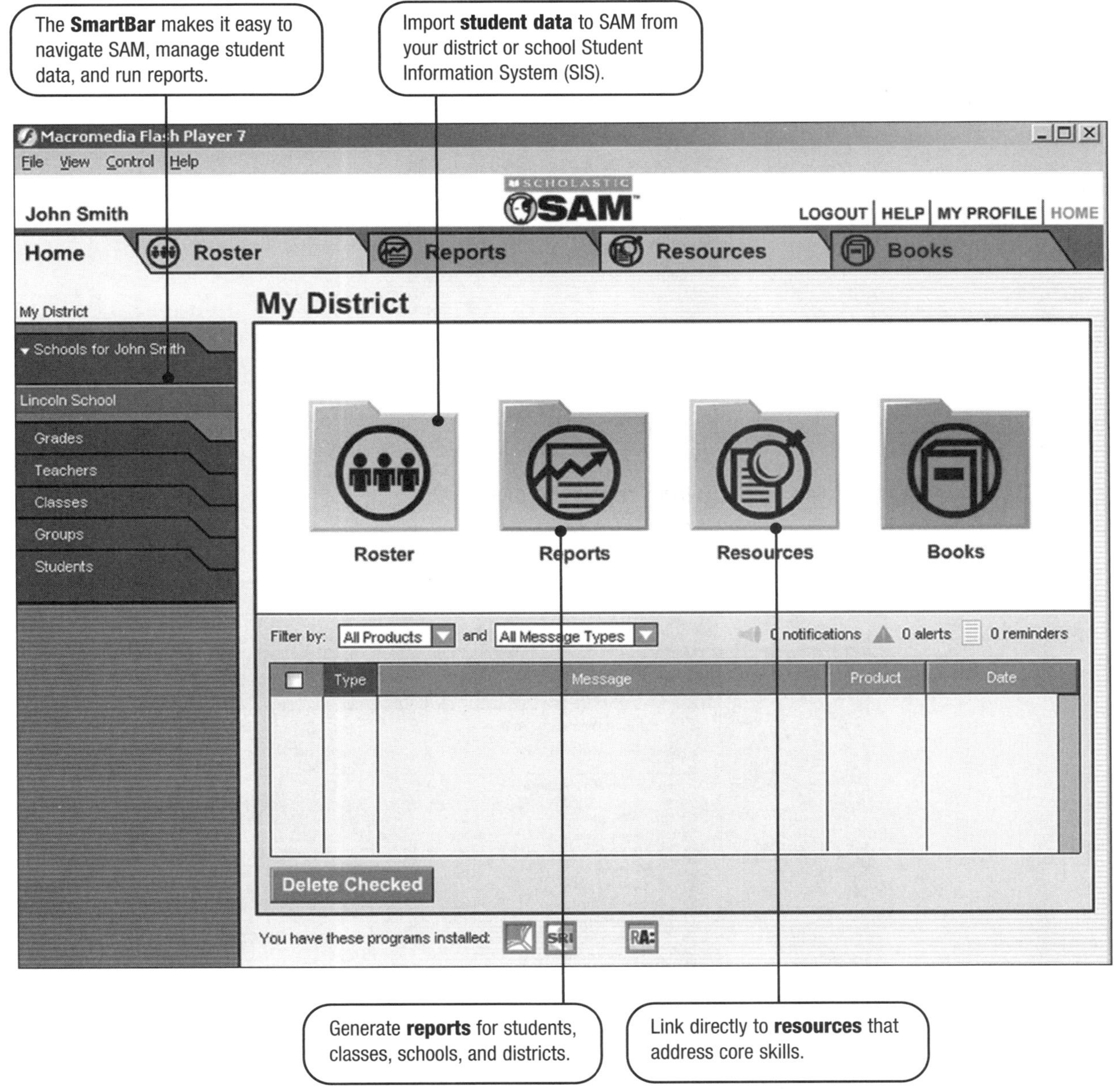

Actionable Reports

SAM reports support you in making daily instructional decisions and communicating reading progress to other staff, principals, teachers, families, and students.

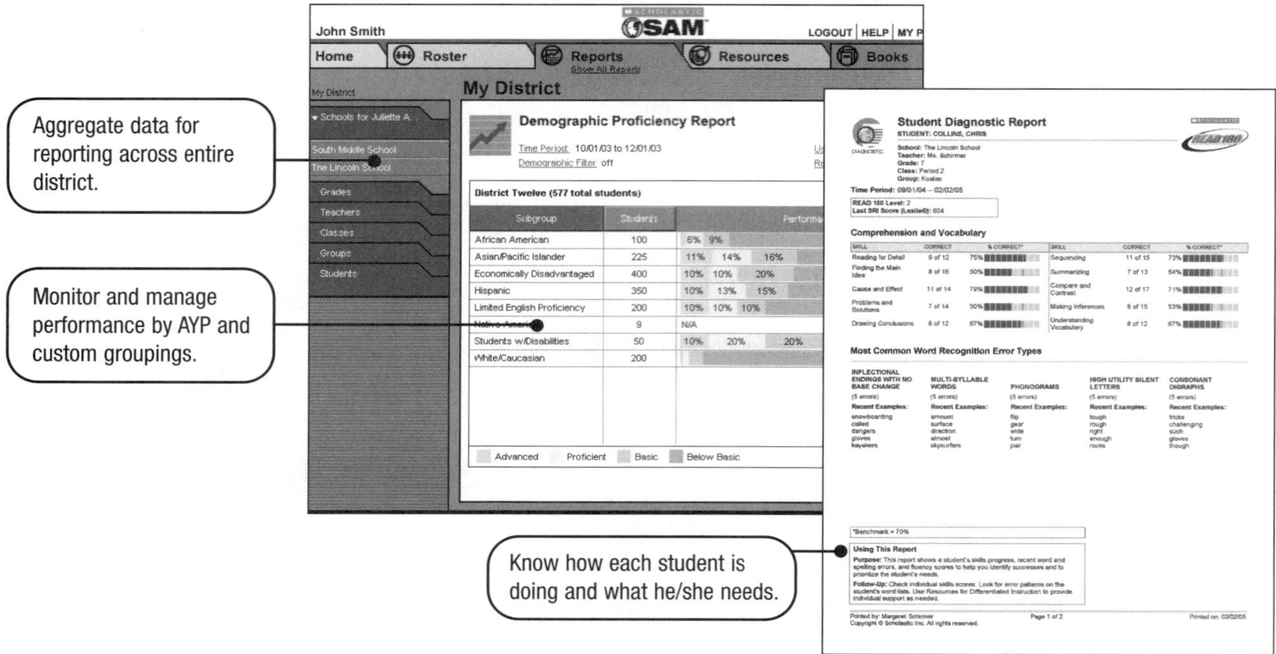

SAM Resources

Using SAM, teachers can link directly from reports to over 2000 resources for differentiating instruction.

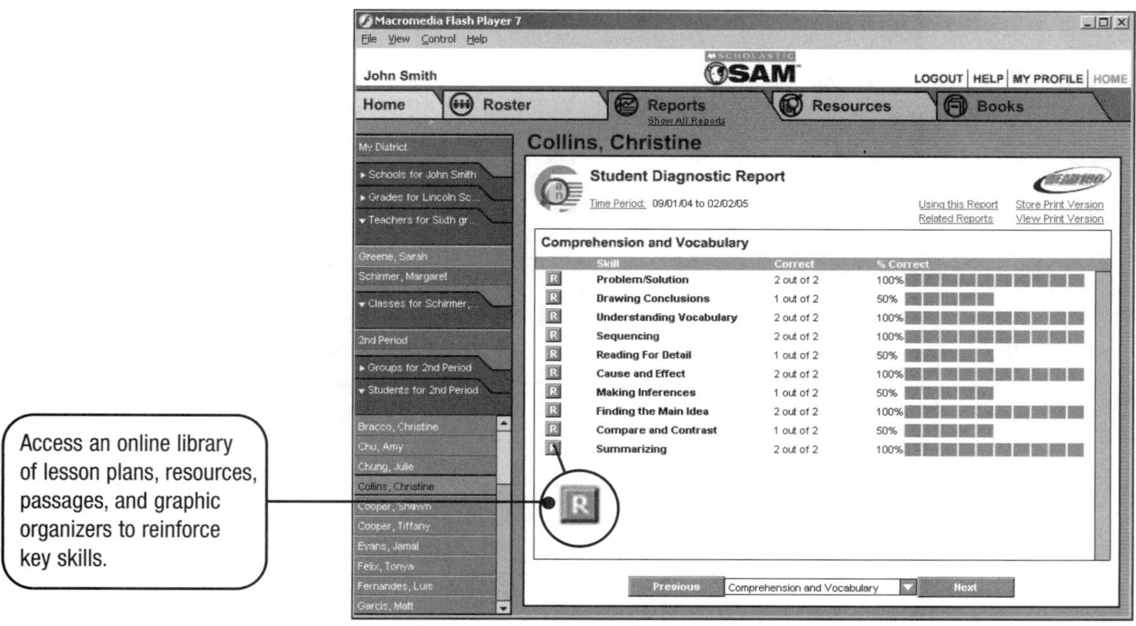

Shared Reading With the *READ 180 rBook*

The *rBooks* are engaging, interactive texts that introduce essential skills and strategies through content-area reading, vocabulary, writing, and grammar instruction.
Each *rBook* includes nine Workshops that require about three weeks each for a complete year of instruction.

- Workshops are taught in sequence.
- Pacing can be adjusted according to student needs.
- Checkpoints are used for differentiated instruction.

rBook Topics (Stage B)

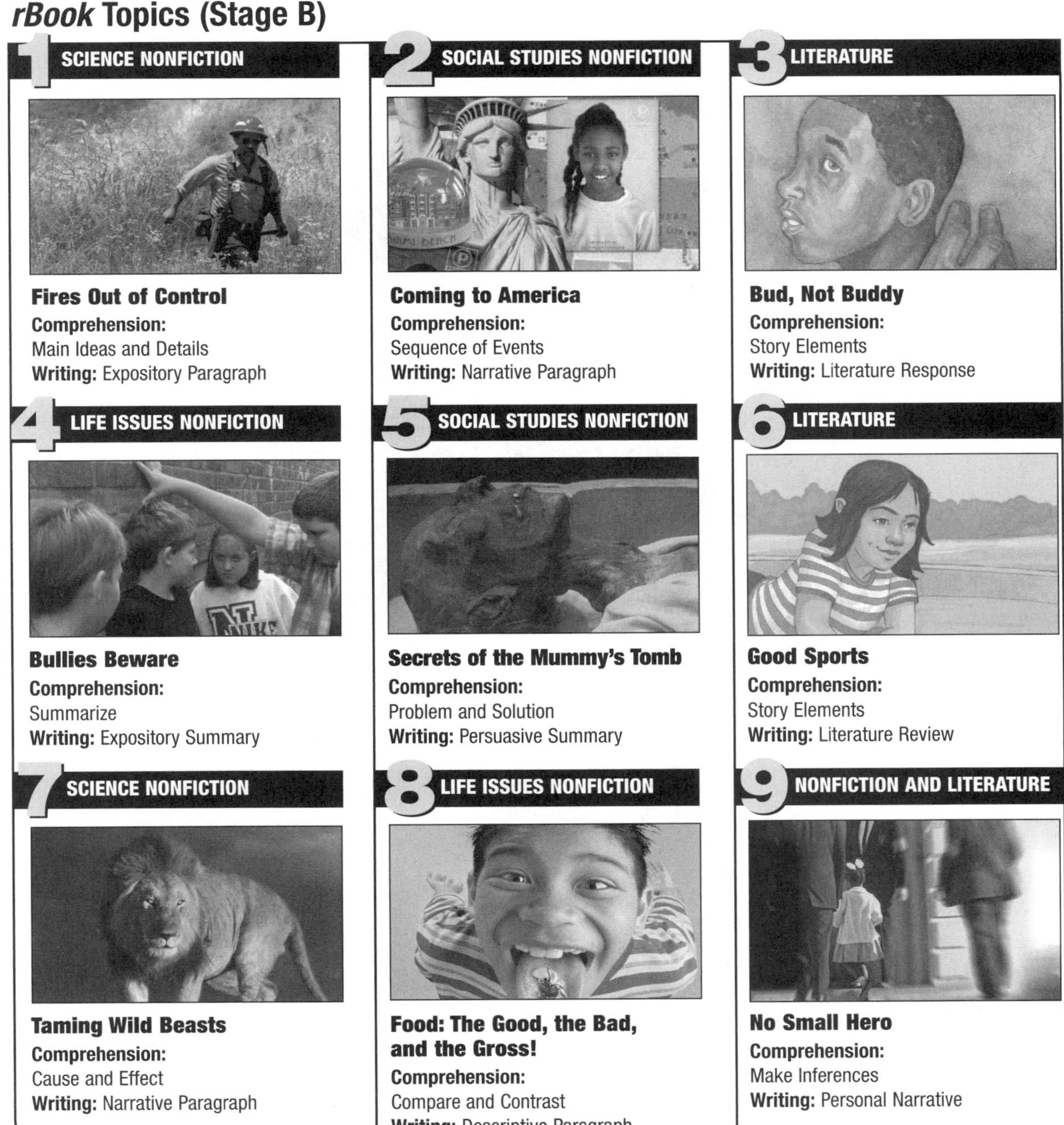

rBook Teaching System

Research has shown that *READ 180* is most effective when used for 90 minutes each day, following the program's proven Instructional Model. The **rBook** provides a clear instructional path for Whole- and Small-Group Instruction, including:

- Explicit teaching and modeling strategies for reading, vocabulary, comprehension, writing, and grammar.

- Research-based routines to build academic language and ensure student engagement.

- Strategic checkpoints that explain when and how to provide data-driven, differentiated instruction.

Stage A (Elementary)

Stage B (Middle School)

Stage C (High School)

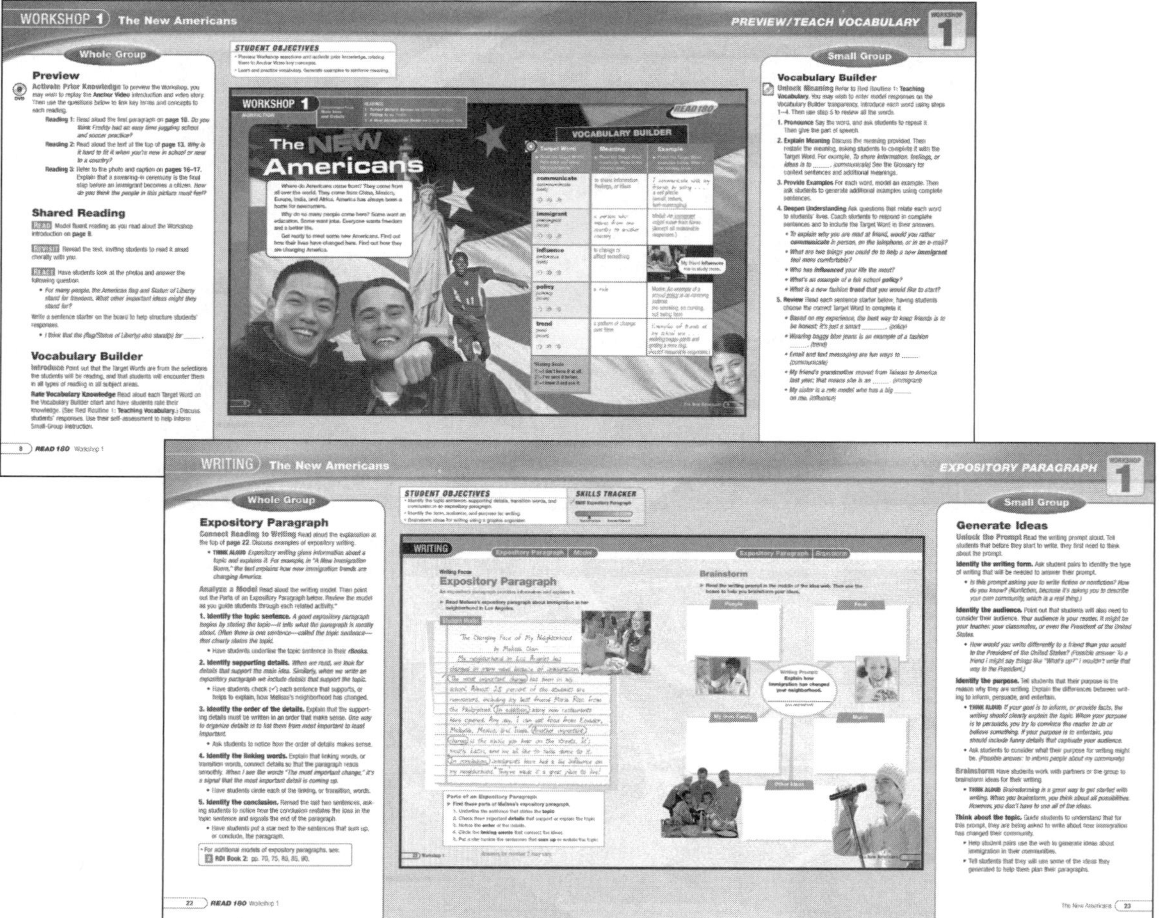

Planning *READ 180* Implementation

Specially developed reading materials, instructional tools, and software offer *READ 180* students a variety of learning opportunities. Over a decade of research has conclusively shown that when schools implement and follow the *READ 180* Instructional Model, significant gains can be expected after one to two years of program participation.

- The *READ 180* Implementation Time Line
- *READ 180* District and School Commitments
- The *READ 180* Instructional Model
- Scheduling Options
- Core Technology Overview
- *READ 180* System Requirements
- The *READ 180* Classroom
- Preparing the *READ 180* Classroom
- Selecting *READ 180* Teachers
- Student Selection and Enrollment

The *READ 180* Implementation Time Line

To make implementation as smooth as possible, Scholastic has developed a time line and a checklist to guide the implementation team. The following time line provides a simple outline of the tasks required during each phase of implementation. Each phase is organized into key components: Partnership & Communication, Technology, Materials, Training & Professional Development, Instruction, Assessment & Evaluation, and In-Classroom Support.

	6 months to 4 weeks before school	**2 to 4 weeks before school**
	PLANNING PHASE	**START-UP PHASE**
Partnership & Communication	• Observe model site • Select *READ 180* coordinator • Identify student selection criteria • Organize district stakeholders meeting	• Present Implementation Plan (S) • Initiate parent communication
Technology	• Technical Requirements Audit (S)* • Select Technical Support Plan	• Install software • Phone/email check-in post-installation (S) • Technical Training (S)
Materials	• Identify number of students, schools, classrooms, stages • Order materials	• Ship materials (S) • Unpack
Training & Professional Development	• Identify number of teachers • Select *READ 180* Seminars • Schedule Training & Seminar Dates (S)	• Attend Day 1 Teacher Training (S) • Enroll in Scholastic Online Professional Development • Leadership Training (S)
Instruction	• Identify teacher criteria • Review school schedules	• Import/enroll students in SAM • Set Up classrooms • Begin lesson planning
Assessment & Evaluation	• Review student enrollment and criteria • Develop District Research Plan	→
In-Classroom Support	• Select and prepare dedicated *READ 180* classrooms	→

*(S) Provided by, or in collaboration with, Scholastic.

SCHOOL YEAR 1

| Weeks 1–3 | Weeks 4–26 | Weeks 27–40 |

| **IN-CLASSROOM PHASE** | | **END-OF-YEAR PHASE** |

- Ongoing contact between *READ 180* Coordinator, Principals, and Teachers ⟶
- *READ 180* Newsletter (S)

- Phone/email/Web tech support (S)
- Provide on-site technical support as needed (S) ⟶
- Backup database (continuous)

- Export & aggregate data

- Additional materials as needed ⟶

- Pack & secure *READ 180* materials
- Reorder missing/damaged materials

- Attend Day 2 Teacher Training (S)
- Attend *READ 180* Seminars (S) ⟶
- Enroll in online Professional Development: Best Practices for Reading Intervention (S)

- Attend *READ 180* Institute (Summer)

- Introduce *READ 180*
- Model rotations and routines
- Show Teacher/Student Video
- Initiate Parent communication

- Diagnose & differentiate instructional needs
- Monitor student progress with SAM ⟶

- Schedule SRI Test Window 1
- Perform Data Analysis

- Monitor SRI Test Windows 2 and/or 3
- *READ 180* Reporting
- Perform Data Analysis

- Monitor Final SRI Test Window
- Complete End of Year Reports
- Consider student exit criteria

- Check in for classroom setup (S)

- Check in for implementation levels (S)

- Check in for end of year planning (S)

READ 180 District and School Commitments

To assure a smooth implementation and start-up, Scholastic has developed a comprehensive *READ 180* partnership plan for Communication, Materials Planning, Technology, Training & Professional Development, Instruction, Assessment & Evaluation, and In-Classroom Support. Each component also fits into phases to help manage the *READ 180* implementation partnership.

There are four phases to *READ 180* Implementation:

1. Planning Phase
2. Start-Up Phase
3. In-Classroom Phase
4. Results Phase

Below are key steps to getting started with the implementation that can be used as a Checklist.

Planning Phase (6 months to 4 weeks before school year begins)

Critical steps of the Planning Phase include assuring that the necessary materials, equipment, dates, and personnel are in place before implementation occurs.

❏ Observe a *READ 180* Model Site.

❏ Hold a meeting for district stakeholders, including Technology, Curriculum, Instruction, and Research.

❏ Select a *READ 180* Coordinator.

❏ Determine the number of schools, classrooms, and teachers.

❏ Provide classrooms with sufficient space for the *READ 180* rotations.

❏ Schedule 90 minutes daily of uninterrupted student contact time in the *READ 180* class.

❏ Schedule Technology Audits.

❏ Select a Technology Support Plan.

❏ Order *READ 180* and secure appropriate technology needs and materials (teacher workstation, printer, overhead projector, TV with DVD player, 5–7 CD players and enough computers for 1/3rd of students in the class per *READ 180* classroom).

❏ Select *READ 180* teachers.

❏ Use a student selection process that includes multiple measures to ensure appropriate placement, keeping each *READ 180* classroom to 15–21 students.

❏ Schedule training and professional development.

❏ Discuss questions to form basis of District Research Plan.

Start-Up Phase (2–4 weeks before school)

The start-up phase should be around or close to the start of the school calendar.

❏ Unpack materials.

❏ Install the *READ 180* technology.

❏ Attend Scholastic's training and professional development.

❏ Enroll in Red course.

❏ Set up *READ 180* classrooms (supply furniture for the small-group rotations and enough outlets for the computer workstations).

❏ Inform parents of selected students about *READ 180.*

❏ Enroll students in *Scholastic Achievement Manager* (SAM).

❏ Begin planning lessons.

In-Classroom Phase (Weeks 1–26)

The *READ 180* teaching materials and reports provide content and direction for teachers to teach and differentiate instruction with the program.

❏ Begin instruction using *READ 180* materials and instructional model.

❏ Administer the Scholastic Reading Inventory 2–3 times.

❏ Attend Scholastic's training and professional development.

❏ Back-up data on SAM (ongoing).

❏ Report progress to students, parents, and district.

❏ Order additional materials as needed.

❏ Monitor implementation and student progress.

Results Phase (Weeks 27–40)

❏ Administer final Scholastic Reading Inventory.

❏ Aggregate student data.

❏ Analyze student and implementation data.

❏ Report results.

❏ Consider student exit criteria and identify students for next year.

❏ Secure materials.

❏ Re-order missing or damaged materials.

❏ Enroll in *READ 180* Summer Institute and schedule professional development for teachers.

❏ Hold a meeting for district stakeholders, including Technology, Curriculum, Instruction, and Research.

❏ Determine the number of schools, classrooms, and teachers for the following year.

The *READ 180* Instructional Model

An Instructional Model That Works

The *READ 180* Instructional Model provides a simple way to organize instruction and classroom activity. The session begins and ends with Whole-Group Instruction. In between Whole-Group meetings, students break into three small groups that rotate among three stations as shown below.

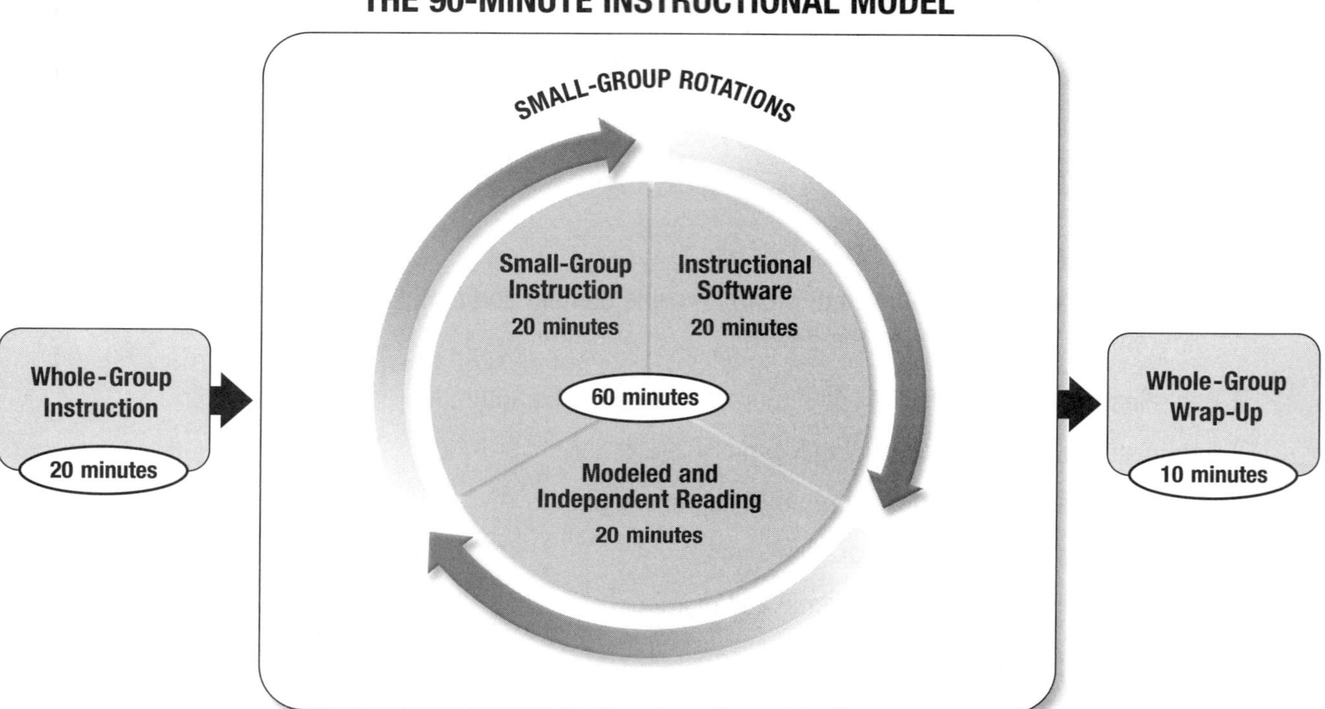

Whole-Group Instruction	Small-Group Rotations			Whole-Group Wrap-Up
Using the *READ 180 rBook* and instructional materials, the teacher begins the session by providing systematic instruction in reading, writing, and vocabulary to the whole class.	**Small-Group Instruction** Using the *rBook* and *Resources for Differentiated Instruction*, the teacher provides diagnostically informed instruction, working closely with students to meet individual needs.	**Instructional Software** Students use the *READ 180* Software independently for intensive, individualized skills practice.	**Modeled and Independent Reading** Students build fluency and reading comprehension skills through modeled and independent reading of *READ 180* Paperbacks and Audiobooks.	The session ends with ten minutes of Whole-Group Wrap-Up.

Scheduling Options

Based on over five years of research in hundreds of school districts, we know that to maximize results, *READ 180* should be scheduled every day for 90 consecutive minutes. Scholastic has developed three options for implementing *READ 180* in middle and high schools. The following examples are for a middle or high school with 60 *READ 180* students:

1) **Option 1 – One dedicated *READ 180* classroom with one *READ 180* teacher.** The school sets up one *READ 180* classroom with one dedicated *READ 180* teacher. Three sections of 20 students per class are scheduled. A total of 60 students will be served.

2) **Option 2 – One dedicated *READ 180* classroom with two *READ 180* teachers.** The school sets up one *READ 180* classroom with two *READ 180* teachers. Each teacher uses the room to teach 15 students at two different times per day. A total of 60 students will be served.

3) **Option 3 – Two dedicated *READ 180* classrooms with two *READ 180* teachers.** The school sets up two *READ 180* classrooms with two dedicated *READ 180* teachers (one in each classroom) teaching 15 students for each 90-minute rotation block. Each teacher teaches two *READ 180* classes per day. A total of 60 students will be served.

If immediate implementation of the 90-minute model is impossible in the first year, flexible implementations such as the following can be used, but are not recommended. Alternate schedules for high schools, such as those below, should include daily use of the Software and class periods of at least 90 minutes to ensure program fidelity, student progress, and the best results.

1. Consecutive 45- or 50-minute class periods

Schedule two 45- or 50-minute classes back-to-back to effectively match the research-proven *READ 180* Instructional Model. This may be accomplished by back-to-back scheduling of a regular Reading/English class period with a study hall, an elective course, or another adjustable class period.

2. Non-consecutive 45- or 50-minute class periods

Schedule two 45- or 50-minute classes per day:

- One Period: The teacher leads 20–25 minutes of Whole-Group Instruction. Then the students divide into three groups and complete one of the regular rotations.

- Other Period: Students complete the two remaining rotations.

3. For schools with block scheduling

Assign one or two classes to alternating 90-minute schedules. For example, with two classes, a schedule such as the following could be established:

- Class A: 90 minutes Monday, Wednesday, and Friday on alternate weeks

- Class B: 90 minutes Tuesday and Thursday on alternate weeks

If possible, students can work on *READ 180* Software daily in a computer lab or other location before, during, or after school.

4. 45- or 50-minute class, plus computer lab

- Students complete 20–30 minutes of daily supervised work on the Software outside of class.

- The teacher leads the class in Whole-Group Direct Instruction for two full periods per week.

- On other days, students complete the two remaining rotations: 1) Small-Group Instruction and 2) Modeled and Independent Reading.

- To keep groups small in size, a writing rotation may be added. This may be accomplished by subdividing the Small-Group Instruction rotation, where half of the students complete writing assignments while the rest of the students meet with the teacher. The groups switch places halfway through the 20–25 minute rotation.

5. Use after school and in summer school

READ 180 may be implemented effectively in after-school and summer school programs, both for students who use the program daily and for others. Scholastic can work with you to design schedules for these types of programs.

> **With three rotations in a class period students remain engaged and motivated because they are constantly moving and starting something different with each new rotation.—Lori Lambert, District Reading Facilitator, Huntington Beach, CA**

Core Technology Overview

The *Scholastic Achievement Manager* (SAM) is the management system and new technology platform for all Scholastic Enterprise Edition (EE) applications. Previous versions of Scholastic products were supported by the Scholastic Management System (SMS).

The Enterprise Edition takes advantage of advances in technology, addresses the needs of schools created by the introduction of NCLB, and provides a platform for the district-wide implementation of Scholastic products. The new technology platform provides district administrators and technology directors with the ability to implement and monitor applications on a district-wide basis and it provides teachers with improved data-driven instruction. It also provides district-wide capabilities such as district reporting, AYP demographic grouping and reporting, and AYP demographic filtering.

SAM Technology Platform

SAM is built using pure Internet and industry-standard technology. Its main components include:

- MySQL, the world's most widely used open-source database.
- JBoss, the leading open source, standards-compliant, J2EE-based application server implemented in 100% pure Java.
- JDK, the standard edition Java 2 Platform.
- JRE, Java Runtime Environment, the technology that allows users to run Java applications.
- Apache, the most widely available Web server on the Internet.
- XML, Extensible Markup Language, a simple, very flexible data interchange format.

The new technology of SAM provides changes in three key areas: improved performance, districtwide capabilities with enhanced data-handling features, and data-driven instruction.

Improved Performance

SAM is built to provide for high levels of concurrent usage within the bounds of typical school infrastructures and capabilities. A single application server is capable of supporting large numbers of concurrent users. For example, in one of our tests using Windows 2000 workstations on a local area network, 50 *READ 180* students, 150 SRI students, and 10 teachers were all able to use Enterprise applications running off of a single SAM server (Windows, 2003, single processor with 2GB RAM), simultaneously with no noticeable decrease in performance. This represents approximately 15 classrooms using Enterprise applications at the same time. The exact performance you can expect will be affected by many factors, including:

- The hardware supporting your applications.
- The infrastructure in place in your district.
- The various other applications that consume different amounts of system resources and bandwidth.

Be sure to consult Scholastic Technical Services at 1-888-557-7299 about your particular usage and infrastructure when planning to deploy the Enterprise Edition.

Enterprise Edition Recommended System Requirements

Computer	Platform	Operating System (with latest Service Packs)	Processor	Memory	Free hard Disk Space	Other	Internet Access
Student Workstation	Windows	Windows XP SP2	Pentium IV/1.0GHz	256 MB	500 MB	QuickTime 16-bit sound card, headphones, microphone	No
	Macintosh	Mac OS X v10.4.3 (See notes 8 and 9)	G4/1.25GHz				
Teacher or Administrator Workstation	Windows	Windows XP SP2	Pentium IV/1.5GHz	512 MB	500 MB	QuickTime 16-bit sound card, Acrobat Reader, headphones, browser	Yes
	Macintosh	Mac OS X v10.4.3 (See notes 8 and 9)	G4/1.25GHz				
Application Server	Windows	Windows 2003 Server	Dual 3.2 GHz Xeon	2048 MB	5 GB	The installer will configure the server with correct versions of MySQL, JBoss, and JRE.	Yes
	Macintosh	Mac OS X v10.4 Xserve G5	Dual 2.0 GHz G5				
Data Aggregation Server (Optional)	Windows	Windows 2003 Server	Dual 3.2 GHz Xeon	2048 MB	1 GB per school (does not include student recordings)		Yes
	Macintosh	Mac OS X v10.4 Xserve G5	Dual 2.0 GHz G5				

System Requirements and Performance

1. SAM servers require a fixed IP address, or Domain Name Server (DNS). Please see the *READ 180 Installation and Troubleshooting Guide* for information on configuring SAM when using DHCP.
2. Overall system performance, including number of concurrent users, is affected by network bandwidth, server memory, processor speed, disk drive performance, and many other factors. Please see the *READ 180 Installation and Troubleshooting Guide* for information on configuring SAM for best performance.
3. Scholastic strongly recommends SAM be installed on a dedicated server that is not used by other applications. If SAM is installed on a server shared with other applications, overall system memory and disk space requirements will vary according to the needs of the other programs.
4. The following Internet Browsers are supported (required for performing certain administrative tasks involving data import and export): On Windows, Internet Explorer 5.x, 6.x, and 7.x. On Mac OS 9, Internet Explorer 5.1. On Mac OS X, Safari 1.2.
5. Workstations and Servers require a Network Interface Card supporting TCP/IP. Wireless networks (802.11a or 802.11g) are supported but are limited to the bandwidth capacity of your wireless network.

Operating System

1. The Enterprise products have been certified to work on the following Servers: Windows 2000 Server and Windows 2003 Server with PIII or higher processor. Mac OS X v10.3.x and OS X v10.4.x Server with G5 or higher processor. Enterprise Edition programs on Mac OS X run in Native mode and therefore do not require support for Classic mode.
2. The following servers are not supported: Windows 98, ME, and NT; Mac OS X Server v10.0–10.2; Novell 4.x, 5.x, 6.x and OES.
3. The Enterprise products have been certified to work on the following Workstations: Windows 98SE, Windows 2000 Professional, Windows XP. Professional with PIII or higher processor. Mac OS v9.2.2, Mac OS X v10.2.8, Mac OS X v10.3.x, and Mac OS X v10.4.3 with G4 or higher processor.
4. The following workstations are not supported: Windows 95, 98 1st Ed., CE, NT, ME, 2000 Home; XP Home. Mac OS 8.0 to 9.1, Mac OS X v10.0–v10.2.7, Mac OS X v10.4–v10.4.2.

Other

1. DVD drive required for loading ReadAbout content onto an Application Server or Media Server (ReadAbout only).
2. Media (CD- or DVD-based content) may be copied to the hard drives on the student workstations, installed on the Application Server, or installed on a Media Server (any NAS device). *READ 180* requires 5 GB of free hard disk space for content. ReadAbout requires approximately 5 GB.
3. A television and DVD player or a computer with a DVD drive is required for viewing the *rBook* Anchor Videos. Also, 5 portable CD players with headphones are required for the Enterprise Edition Audiobooks (*READ 180* only).
4. Color printers are recommended for Servers and Teacher workstations, but a laser printer will be fine.
5. Student, teacher, and administrator workstations; application servers, and data aggregation servers all require a CD-ROM drive.

The *READ 180* Classroom

An effective *READ 180* classroom is a special place with distinct areas for each rotation for reading, learning, and sharing ideas.

Sample Classroom

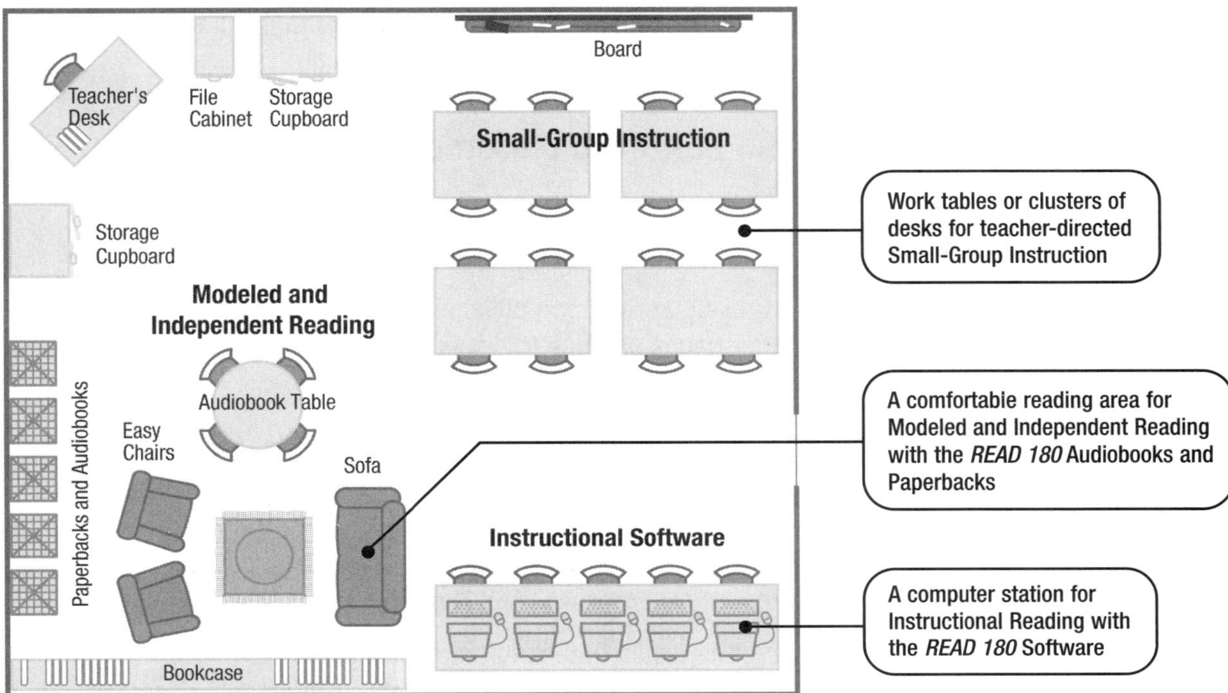

The First Three Weeks

The first three weeks in a *READ 180* classroom are critical in creating a strong first impression and the tone for learning. It is important to support principals and teachers during this critical time by:

- Working with teachers to select appropriate students for *READ 180*.

- Providing resources for teachers to set up their *READ 180* classrooms.

- Communicating with families about the *READ 180* program.

- Scheduling an SRI time frame for all teachers to administer the SRI three to four times per year.

- Checking student profiles in SAM to make sure that the required information is entered in order to monitor student progress.

- Checking an SRI report after the first test to review student Lexile levels and to become familiar with SAM.

- Visiting *READ 180* classrooms to check that they have been set up properly and they have the necessary materials (see page 48).

- Confirming the Implementation Time Line with principals and teachers.

Preparing the *READ 180* Classroom

The setup of a *READ 180* classroom will be the students' first impression of what this program offers them. There is only one chance to create the first impression of the classroom. Ensure the classroom décor is inviting the student to learn. The room should have positive messages about reading and the learning process posted on the walls. The students should see print everywhere. When the student looks in the door, he or she should see books that will target their interests. The *READ 180* classroom is a place where students want to be.

Suggestions for Setting Up the *READ 180* Classroom

Materials

- ❑ 6' tables (5)
- ❑ 1 *READ 180* Student *rBook* per student
- ❑ Bookshelves
- ❑ CD players (5–7)
- ❑ CD storage
- ❑ Comfortable furniture such as beanbag chairs
- ❑ Computer chairs (10)
- ❑ Computer headsets (5–7)
- ❑ Computers (5–7)
- ❑ Microphones (5–7)
- ❑ *READ 180* Audiobook Collection
- ❑ *READ 180* Paperback Collection
- ❑ *READ 180* QuickStart Kit (Posters, Banner, timer)
- ❑ *READ 180* Teacher Bookshelf (5 sections)
- ❑ *READ 180* Topic Software
- ❑ Resealable plastic bags
- ❑ Rotation labels/signs
- ❑ Rules and procedures poster(s)
- ❑ Storage for independent reading
- ❑ Student chairs (10)
- ❑ Vertical files for reproducibles

- Provide a room of good size that offers movement and allows the students to engage fully in *READ 180*.

- Provide at least two bulletin boards: one for seasonal messages and one to display students' successes and publish students' work.

- Place a bulletin board outside of the *READ 180* classroom door so that students can share their published work with others in the school.

- Position the teacher's desk off to the side or in a corner of the *READ 180* classroom. The focus is then on the students.

- Set up distinct areas for each part of the *READ 180* rotation. The three main areas of the *READ 180* classroom are labeled: Modeled and Independent Reading area, Instructional Software area, and Small-Group area.

- Support a teacher who may want to provide a different atmosphere for each station. The Modeled and Independent Reading area has comfortable furniture, the Instructional Software area is separate to allow students to make their recordings, and the Small-Group area has a table for group work.

- Create posters with positive reading messages.

- Collect baskets, crates, jars, tins, and boxes to store materials. Use the baskets for themed books, batteries and chargers.

- Visit thrift stores and garage sales for comfortable furniture for the Modeled and Independent Reading area.

- Develop a book checkout system.

- Plan an area for storing journals and writing portfolios.

Selecting *READ 180* Teachers

READ 180 teachers should be chosen primarily for their commitment to struggling students and to believing that all students can become successful readers. Additionally, the right *READ 180* teacher:

The right *READ 180* teacher:

- Has the desire to work with older, struggling students.
- Believes that these students can and will become successful readers.
- Has high expectations for all students.
- Makes a commitment to implement the *READ 180* Instructional Model.
- Has strong classroom management skills.
- Understands that the older student is motivated by respect, choice, and safety.
- Has a desire to learn about teaching the reading and writing process.
- Has a commitment to continued professional development.
- Possesses a positive attitude.
- Is flexible with instruction—using whole-group, small-group, and one-on-one as necessary.
- Is committed to providing a print-rich environment within the classroom.
- Is committed to teaching with the "to, with, and by" model of literacy instruction.
- Is dedicated to individualized instruction.
- Is comfortable with multiple learning groups occurring at the same time in the classroom.
- Is dedicated to utilizing technology to support the reading and writing process.

Student Selection and Enrollment

Selecting Students

READ 180 is designed to help struggling readers improve their reading ability, experience success in completing reading tasks, and boost their interest of reading. Students who can benefit most from the *READ 180* program should be selected based on each school or district's needs and population.

Scholastic recommends that you use the Scholastic Reading Inventory (SRI) test among other measures to identify *READ 180* candidates. SRI is a computer-adaptive test that assesses reading comprehension using the Lexile Framework, a system that measures readers and texts on the same scale.

Other signs that students might benefit from *READ 180* include:

- Student performance on tests indicates that a student is in the bottom two quartiles.
- Student proficiency exams show that a student is reading below grade level.
- Teacher observation and assessments show that a student is reading below grade level and is in need of intervention.
- Student who is an English-Language Learner reading below grade level.
- Student who is in Special Education program and is in need of reading intervention.

Enrolling Students

READ 180 has four instructional levels (three in Stage A) to accommodate a wide range in reading proficiencies. Placement in the correct *READ 180* level enables each student to practice reading and build phonics, fluency, vocabulary, spelling and comprehension skills using texts that are engaging, content-rich, and appropriately challenging. The following table shows grade level reading equivalents for *READ 180* Stages A, B, and C.

Three Stages of Instruction and Support

READ 180 Level	Elementary Stage A Transitional 3–6	Middle School Stage B Grades 6–8	High School Stage C Grade 9 and above
Level 1	1.5 to 2.5*	1.5 to 2.5	1.5 to 2.5
Level 2	2.5 to 4.0	2.5 to 4.0	2.5 to 4.0
Level 3	4.0 to 6.9	4.0 to 6.0	4.0 to 6.0
Level 4		6.0 to 8.9	6.0 to 12.0

*Denotes reading level

Students are placed in the appropriate *READ 180* level using the SRI test. The *Scholastic Achievement Manager* (SAM) provides each student's SRI result as a Lexile® score. Based on their initial SRI scores, SAM then places each student in the appropriate *READ 180* level to begin the program. Teachers and administrators can override SAM's automatic placement as needed.

Supporting *READ 180* Classrooms

Once a *READ 180* classroom is operating, we need to support teachers to be successful. In this section, we suggest ways to build a community to support *READ 180* teachers, evaluate and observe *READ 180* implementation, seek technical support, and plan for what to do when a teacher is unavailable.

- **Building a *READ 180* Teacher Community**
- **Evaluating Implementation**
- **Observing a *READ 180* Classroom: Survey**
- **Observing a *READ 180* Classroom: Protocol**
- ***READ 180* Technical Support Services**
- **Planning for Substitutes**
- **Student Exit Criteria**

Building a *READ 180* Teacher Community

READ 180 teachers benefit greatly from sharing ideas, knowledge and best practices to increase student results. The program provides a range of ways to build a teacher community. Whether there are a couple or many teachers per school building, the following tools and suggestions can assist in creating a community for *READ 180* teachers.

READ 180 Community Web Site: www.read180.com

With everything from the latest reading intervention research to interviews with the program's author to chat forums, the *READ 180* Community Web site offers a vast array of services and support, including:

- Tips for new teachers.
- Correlations to state standards.
- "Ask Noelle"—answers to questions from a master *READ 180* teacher.
- Printable parent letters and student achievement certificates.
- Strategies for using *READ 180* reports to differentiate instruction.
- Frequently asked questions on hardware troubleshooting.

Regular Cadre Meetings

Many successful *READ 180* implementations use regular (monthly) meetings to support new and continuing *READ 180* teachers. Meetings can be organized and led by the school district or Scholastic, so that teachers gain support from sharing experiences and connecting to what is happening in other classrooms in their district. Meeting agendas can include:

- Setting up the *READ 180* Classroom
- *READ 180* Classroom Management
- *READ 180* Technical Support
- Scholastic Professional Development Opportunities
- Using the *READ 180* Reports
- Student Grouping
- Managing Small-Group Instruction
- Managing Independent Reading Rotation
- Data Collection
- Assessment and Grading
- Using Lexiles

Scholastic Red Discussion Boards

The Red discussion boards on the online course at www.ScholasticRed.com are bulletin boards in which messages are left, or "posted," to be read by any participating learner at any time. Teachers taking the online course can click on a discussion subject and view responses or contribute one of their own.

Intranet/Local Discussions/Chats

To provide continuous support to *READ 180* teachers, Scholastic recommends setting up a local, electronic discussion group. This can be achieved through an already existing Intranet, an email application with discussion folders, or the district Web site. This provides teachers with another opportunity to be a part of a local *READ 180* community.

Evaluating Implementation

A quick evaluation of the implementation level of a *READ 180* classroom can help administrators anticipate the gains that will be seen by *READ 180* students and reveal the need for more in-depth evaluation in some classrooms. The following sets of indicators can be used to define program implementation levels of *READ 180*. For purposes of research and reporting, Level 1 defines full implementation, and Levels 2 and 3 define incomplete implementation. Implementation that does not at least meet the standard suggested by Level 3 should be considered as not implementing *READ 180*.

Level 1 Full Implementation: all indicators (1–10)

Level 2 Implementation: indicators 2–7, plus any combination of indicators 8–10

Level 3 Implementation: indicators 3–6, plus any combination of indicators 7–10

☐ Yes	☐ No	1. Class schedule includes 90-minute blocks five days a week beginning each class with 20 minutes of Whole-Group Instruction and ending with 10 minutes of Whole-Group Instruction.
☐ Yes	☐ No	2. Class schedule includes three 20-minute rotations five days a week with no more than five to seven students per group.
☐ Yes	☐ No	3. Sufficient working hardware, computers, headphones, and CD players for all students to pass through the rotations each day the class meets.
☐ Yes	☐ No	4. Adequate sets of *READ 180* **rBooks**, Paperbacks, Audiobooks, CDs, and Topic Software.
☐ Yes	☐ No	5. Adequate training, professional development, and technical support to facilitate use of the program model.
☐ Yes	☐ No	6. Appropriate configurations of furniture and equipment, including: teacher workstation, independent reading area, computer stations, and Whole/Small-Group Instruction areas. The furniture and equipment is arranged for comfort and ease of mobility.
☐ Yes	☐ No	7. Frequent (at least every 2–3 weeks) teacher use of the *Scholastic Achievement Manager* for tracking and monitoring student progress and reports.
☐ Yes	☐ No	8. Regular teacher use of *READ 180 Teacher's Edition* and of reproducibles contained in *READ 180* instructional materials.
☐ Yes	☐ No	9. Administration of the SRI at the beginning, midpoint, and end of the period of student participation in *READ 180*.
☐ Yes	☐ No	10. Student scheduled for participation in *READ 180* for at least a year.

Observing a *READ 180* Classroom: Survey

Teacher _________________________________ **Grade** _________________________________

School _________________________________ **Observer Name** _________________________________

This observation survey is designed to gauge the fidelity of implementation to the *READ 180* model. A quick evaluation of the implementation level of a *READ 180* classroom can help administrators anticipate the gains that will be seen by *READ 180* students and reveal the need for more in-depth evaluation in some classrooms. It is not intended to be used as part of teacher evaluations.

The survey is for use by a *READ 180* specialist, district administrator, teacher observing the program, or any other instructional leader to gather information about program implementation.

The survey should be shared with teachers before and after a classroom visit to communicate the level of implementation. The points and scale are a suggestion and can be used to compare a classroom at different points of the school year or to compare across classrooms.

Over a decade of research demonstrates that on-model implementation produces significant student results. Data collected with this survey can be used to look at the quality of implementation.

Instructions for using the survey:

1. Show the survey to the teacher. Discuss that the purpose is to collect actionable data to create an ideal *READ 180* implementation. Explain that the survey is not intended to be a part of teacher evaluation.

2. Observe a full 90-minutes class. Note that each part of implementation is separate and that the points should not be totaled for a teacher score.

3. Discuss any part of the survey with the teacher that was not immediately observed.

4. Sit with the teacher after the class, at a later date, or during the next cadre meeting to discuss the observation and ways to improve each part of implementation based on stated outcomes.

Comments:

____

____

____

____

____

____

____

Implementation Survey

Points	0	1	2	3	4	Score
Environment • Schedule • Room Arrangement	Class is completely off-model with no rotations. No defined areas for Small-Group, Modeled and Independent reading, or computers.	Class follows a schedule with inconsistent rotations. Partial group areas present.	Class follows some rotations. Three areas present for rotations.	Class follows whole group, rotations, and wrap-up. Three clearly defined areas present for rotations with procedures posted.	Whole-group, rotations and wrap-up. Clear signal and smooth transitions. Three distinct areas present: comfortable reading area, computers with adequate space between workstations, and table for Small-Group Instruction.	
Whole-Group Instruction	No evidence.	No student engagement.	Activity with little student engagement.	Shared reading with student involvement.	Shared reading with think alouds and modeling and use of academic language.	
Small-Group Instruction • Differentiated Instruction	No rationale for grouping.	Grouping not based on instructional needs; no modification of instruction.	Groupings based on instructional needs; no modification of instruction.	Groupings based on instructional needs; some success modifying instruction.	Groupings based on instructional needs; modification of instruction to meet student needs.	
• Checking for Understanding	No evidence of checking for understanding.	Limited checking for understanding.	Occasional checking for understanding.	Clear checking for understanding.	Consistent and clear checking for understanding.	
Instructional Software	No time for Instructional Software.	Instructional Software time shortened and/or misused.	Instructional Software time misused.	Instructional Software time used for intended purpose, poor student engagement.	Instructional Software time used for intended purpose, students fully engaged on READ 180 Software.	
Modeled and Independent Reading • Student Engagement	No evidence.	Fake Reading.	Students reading.	Students reading appropriate leveled text.	Students reading appropriate leveled text, log entries and quizzes.	
• Reading Area	No clear Modeled and Independent Reading area.	Modeled and Independent Reading area, books not leveled.	Modeled and Independent Reading area, with leveled text.	Modeled and Independent Reading area, with leveled text – some direction for selecting books.	Modeled and Independent Reading area, print rich environment posted information about text and Lexiles.	
Wrap-Up	No wrap-up.	Clean-up only.	Teacher and students review learning.	Teacher and students review skills and/or content learned.	Teacher and students connect skills and/or content learned with stated outcomes and to other content area or classes.	
Use of Data	No use of data.	Limited evidence of use of data.	Some use of data to group students.	Use of data to group students and some differentiation of instruction.	Consistent use of data to group students and differentiate instruction.	

Observing a *READ 180* Classroom: Protocol

Overview

Observing a *READ 180* classroom in-depth can provide good information about the instruction students are receiving from the program. It can also help administrators anticipate the kinds of gains that students are likely to make. This protocol is designed for use by a *READ 180* specialist, district administrator, or any other instructional leader to gather information about program implementation. It is not intended to be used as part of teacher performance appraisals.

The protocol will help answer a variety of questions about *READ 180* implementation within and across classrooms. First and foremost, this protocol is designed to answer the following questions:

- Have teachers fully implemented the *READ 180* program?

- Do all students have equal opportunities to participate in all aspects of the *READ 180* program?

- Are students participating in all components of the *READ 180* program?

- What improvements can the district or school make to support the *READ 180* teacher?

- What additional professional development is necessary to support *READ 180* implementation and instruction?

Data collected with this protocol can also be used to look at the relationship between the quality of implementation and student outcomes.

Definitions of Terms as Used in the Protocol

Comprehension: Students engage in activities designed to foster their capacity to understand or use comprehension skills or strategies. Possible activities include any of the skills addressed by *READ 180* materials—main idea, summarize, sequence of events, read for detail, draw conclusions, make inferences, cause and effect, compare and contrast, problem and solution, analyze character, analyze plot, and analyze setting.

Phonics: Students focus on symbol/sound correspondences, identifying the sounds in words, blending sounds together, decoding letter-by-letter, decoding by onset and rhyme or analogy, or decoding multisyllabic words. Possible activities include any of the phonemic or word structure elements included in *READ 180* materials—high-frequency words, short vowels, long vowels and long-vowel digraphs, consonants that stand for more than one sound, consonant digraphs, consonant clusters, silent consonants, variant vowels, diphthongs, r-controlled vowels, open and closed syllables, syllables with consonant *-le*, schwa, prefixes, suffixes, plurals, inflectional endings with or without base change, compound words, and contractions.

Fluency: Students engage in activities designed to help them recognize words automatically, understand phrasing of text and apply rapid phonic, structural, and contextual analysis to identify unknown words. Students are working toward the goal of reading quickly, in meaningful chunks, and at a high level of accuracy.

Writing: Students engage in the writing process including looking at models of key writing types.

Grammar: Students engage in studying the rules and structure of the English language pertaining to the arrangement of words or generation of sentences.

Vocabulary: Teachers directly teach high-utility academic vocabulary. Students engage in discussing/working on word meaning(s).

Reading Aloud: The teacher reads aloud to the students.

Shared Reading: The teacher reads aloud to the students while the students follow along in their own copy of the same text.

Direct Instruction: The teacher explains concepts or strategies, tells or gives information.

Modeling: The teacher explicitly shows/demonstrates the steps of how to do something or how to do a process as opposed to simply explaining it.

Skills Practice: The teacher engages the students in practicing literacy skills. Skills practice usually involves students working on drills, worksheets, or other "task-oriented" activities that are designed to reinforce previously learned skills.

***The* READ 180 *Research Protocol and Tools* can be used to design and conduct a research study by helping administrators**

- Decide what questions to ask.
- Evaluate *READ 180* implementation.
- Observe *READ 180* classrooms.
- Collect teacher and principal interviews.
- Export student data.

Observing a *READ 180* Classroom: Protocol

Whole-Group Instruction

Observe one complete Whole-Group Instruction rotation and answer the following questions:

1. Fill in this chart with whole numbers:

- Length of Whole-Group Instruction observation _______ minutes

- Length of Whole-Group Instruction rotation _______ minutes

- Number of students participating _______

2. Do the teacher and students discuss homework? ☐ Yes ☐ No

3. Use the following chart to indicate what instructional strategies the teacher is using to cover specific skills. Please enter the number of minutes you observe each instructional element in each box. See pages 56–57 for definitions.

	Reading Aloud	Shared Reading	Direct Instruction	Modeling	Skills Practice	Other
Comprehension						
Phonics						
Fluency						
Writing						
Grammar						
Vocabulary						
Other						

4. During the lesson, does the teacher explicitly speak about the connections between skills taught in the *READ 180* block and other reading tasks (e.g., demands of other classes, reading outside of school, etc.)? ☐ Yes ☐ No

5. Does the teacher appear to assess student understanding of the material on which they are working? ☐ Yes ☐ No

6. Does the teacher use any *READ 180* resources (e.g., *Teacher's Edition,* *rBooks*, and *Resources for Differentiated Instruction*)? ☐ Yes ☐ No

7. If the teacher does use *READ 180* resources, describe them here.

____

8. If the teacher uses other non-*READ 180* resources, describe them here.

____

9. Does the teacher attempt to engage all students in the lesson?
   ☐ Yes, he/she attempts to engage the entire group.
   ☐ No, he/she attempts to engage only some students.
   ☐ No, he/she attempts to engage only one or two students.

10. Did the students appear to be on-task?

    ❏ Yes, all students were on-task.   ❏ Yes, most students were on-task.

    ❏ No, only a few students were on-task.   ❏ No, no students were on-task.

Small-Group Instruction

Observe one complete Small-Group Instruction, and answer the following questions:

11. Fill in this chart with whole numbers:

- Length of Small-Group Instruction observation _______ minutes

- Length of Small-Group Instruction _______ minutes

- Number of students participating _______

12. Use the following chart to indicate what instructional strategies the teacher is using to cover specific skills. Please enter the number of minutes you observe each instructional element in each box. See pags 56–57 for definitions.

	Pre-reading	Shared Reading	Direct Instruction	Modeling	Skills Practice	Other
Vocabulary						
Phonics						
Fluency						
Writing						
Grammar						
Comprehension						
Other						

13. During the lesson, does the teacher explicitly speak about the connections between skills taught in *READ 180* and other reading tasks (e.g., demands of other classes, reading outside of school, etc.)?   ❏ Yes ❏ No

14. Do the students set reading and writing goals?   ❏ Yes ❏ No

15. Does the teacher appear to assess student understanding of the material on which they are working?   ❏ Yes ❏ No

16. Does the teacher use any *READ 180* resources (e.g., **rBooks**, *Resources for Differentiated Instruction* books).   ❏ Yes ❏ No

17. If the teacher does use *READ 180* resources, describe them here.

____

18. If the teacher uses other non-*READ 180* resources, describe them here.

____

19. Does the teacher attempt to engage all students in the lesson?
   ❏ Yes, he/she attempts to engage the entire group.
   ❏ No, he/she attempts to engage only some students.
   ❏ No, he/she attempts to engage only one or two students.

20. Did the students appear to be on-task?
   ❏ Yes, all students were on-task.   ❏ Yes, most students were on-task.
   ❏ No, only a few students were on-task.   ❏ No, no students were on-task.

Instructional Software

Observe ONE group of students working at the Instructional Software and answer the following questions for ONE rotation.

21. Fill in with whole numbers:

   • Length of computer workstation instruction observation _______ minutes

   • Length of computer workstation instruction _______ minutes

   • Number of students participating _______

22. How many students are using the following? (Fill in whole numbers.)

   _______ Headsets _______ Microphones _______ *READ 180* Software

23. How many students are working on the following components of the Software?
(Fill in whole numbers.)
   _______ Spelling Zone _______ Word Zone _______ Reading Zone _______ *rSkills Tests*
   _______ Success Zone _______ *Scholastic Reading Counts!* Program _______ SRI

24. Did the students appear to be on task?
   ❏ Yes, all students were on-task.   ❏ Yes, most students were on-task.
   ❏ No, only a few students were on-task.   ❏ No, no students were on-task.

Modeled and Independent Reading

25. Observe students working at the Modeled and Independent Reading area and answer the following questions for ONE rotation. Fill in with whole numbers:

   • Length of independent reading observation _______ minutes

   • Length of independent reading _______ minutes

   • Number of students participating _______

26. How many students are reading *READ 180* Paperbacks? _______

27. How many students are using *READ 180* Audiobooks? _______

28. If students are using *READ 180* Audiobooks, do most of the students
appear to be listening and following along with the text?   ❏ Yes   ❏ No

29. How many students are engaged in any of the following? (Fill in whole numbers.)

_________ Reading Logs   _________ Teacher conferencing

_________ Reading progress charts   _________ QuickWrites

_________ Reading silently   _________ Reading aloud to a partner

30. Did the students appear to be on-task?

❏ Yes, all students were on-task.   ❏ Yes, most students were on-task.

❏ No, only a few students were on-task.   ❏ No, no students were on-task.

Whole-Group Wrap-Up

Observe Whole-Group Wrap-Up, and answer the following questions:

31. Fill in with whole numbers:

- Length of Whole-Group Wrap-Up observation _________ minutes

- Length of Whole-Group Wrap-Up _________ minutes

- Number of students participating _________

32. Does the teacher attempt to engage all students in the lesson?   ❏ Yes   ❏ No

33. Did the students appear to be on-task?

❏ Yes, all students were on-task.   ❏ Yes, most students were on-task.

❏ No, only a few students were on-task.   ❏ No, no students were on-task.

Classroom Management and Organization

Based on the entire observation of the class, answer the following questions:

34. Are there clear signals to indicate rotation changes?   ❏ Yes   ❏ No

35. How many minutes does each rotation change require?

_________ Rotation 1   _________ Rotation 3

_________ Rotation 2   _________ Rotation 4

36. Are the rotations and transitions smooth (i.e., quiet, orderly)?   ❏ Yes   ❏ No

37. How many assistants or aides are present in the classroom? _________

38. If there are assistants or aides present, what are they doing? (Check all that apply.)

❏ Working with students on instruction   ❏ Providing the teacher with clerical assistance

❏ Providing technical (i.e., computer) assistance   ❏ Other _________________________________

39. How often does the teacher use SAM to monitor student progress?

❏ Not yet/Not available   ❏ Monthy

❏ Daily   ❏ Once per grading period

❏ Weekly   ❏ Once a year

40. How often does the teacher administer the SRI to students? _________________________________

READ 180 Technical Support Services

Scholastic offers technical support services to meet a variety of needs. Please call *READ 180* Customer Support at 1-877-234-READ (7323) from 7:00 A.M. – 6:00 P.M. EST for assistance.

- *READ 180* **Materials** – Software manuals and installation guides are provided with the program and give detailed directions for technical and system administrators and teachers to use all the key programs: *READ 180*, Scholastic Reading Inventory, *Scholastic Reading Counts!*, *rSkills Tests*, and the *Scholastic Achievement Manager*.

- **Standard Support Plan:** an annual technical support plan that entitles you access to:
  - Phone 1-877-234-READ (7323)
  - Email (techsupport@scholastic.com)
  - 24-hour Web support www.read180.com
  - Onsite Visits: a Scholastic Field Technical Manager can visit your school in case you encounter any technical problems using *READ 180* that cannot be resolved over the phone, email, or by remote access.

- **24-Hour Online Suppor**t – Web-based information is available 24 hours a day, 7 days a week by going to <u>www.read180.com</u> and clicking on the *READ 180* Technical Support link. This service is free to everyone. You will find product information, technical resources, discussions, software downloads, frequently asked questions, and much more.

On-Site Technical Training

Scholastic offers in-depth training for your staff to become proficient in supporting the basic technology needs of a *READ 180* classroom. Technology professionals and *READ 180* administrators learn how to perform on-site service on *READ 180* and SAM technology. Topics include: network environments, installation, the *Scholastic Achievement Manager* (SAM), software usage, file architecture, and troubleshooting. Please be advised that there are fees associated with this service.

- **On-site Installation** – *READ 180* is designed to install easily. However, if you do not wish to perform the self-installation, Scholastic can arrange for a Field Technical Manager to install *READ 180* for you. Please be advised that there are fees associated with this service.

- **Additional Technical Services** – Scholastic can discuss other needs you may have to ensure a timely and successful deployment of the *READ 180* program. For example, data import/export, data migration, or data aggregation services. Please be advised that there are fees associated with these services.

Planning for Substitutes

Occasionally, a *READ 180* teacher will be absent and a substitute teacher will need to fill in for him or her. Ideally, this substitute will be able to maintain the *READ 180* model in the teacher's absence. There are several steps you can take as an administrator to help substitutes maintain the *READ 180* model.

Keeping Emergency Substitute Plans

Plan ahead for unexpected absences by having teachers make emergency substitute plans in the beginning of the year. Make sure that they include enough information and lessons for at least three days of school. Keep a substitute folder in the office for each teacher so that they are available in the event of an unplanned absence. Set time throughout the year, such as each grading period, for teachers to add to and update their emergency substitute plans as necessary. Some of the materials you may have teachers include are:

- Lesson plans for three days.
- Classroom management procedures.
- School schedules.
- Class lists.
- Rotation groups.
- Special schedules for individual students.
- School maps.
- School emergency procedures.
- Student medical information.

Dedicating a *READ 180* Substitute

If you have several *READ 180* classrooms within your school or district, you may want to plan ahead by *dedicating a substitute* to be the *READ 180* substitute teacher. To prepare, this teacher could attend *READ 180* trainings, observe *READ 180* classrooms, become familiar with the Instructional Model, and learn the classroom procedures. This way, when a *READ 180* teacher is absent, the substitute is familiar with the program and able to manage the Instructional Model. The students can rotate and participate in the different parts of the Instructional Model as usual.

Maintaining the Model

If students understand the *READ 180* procedures and are well trained to follow the model, the substitute teacher can have them rotate to the different areas during an absence. The *READ 180* teacher will specify lessons or activities for Whole- and Small-Group Instruction. Depending on where the class is within the **rBook** Workshops, the teacher may choose to have the substitute continue with **rBook** instruction, or choose relevant lessons or practice from the *Resources for Differentiated Instruction* books to teach during Whole- and Small-Group Instruction.

You can use page 65 as a handout for substitutes to explain *READ 180* briefly. You may wish to copy page 65 and page 42, the Instructional Model, for all substitute teachers.

Adjusting the Model

If it is the beginning of the year and students are still learning classroom procedures and expectations, or when the substitute is not familiar with the *READ 180* Instructional Model and not comfortable managing students as they rotate to the different areas of the classroom, then the substitute teacher should plan to adjust the model. Here are suggestions based on a 90-minute class period:

Option 1:

- Read aloud from the *READ 180* Library (15 minutes)
- *RDI Book 1* Comprehension lesson or *RDI Book 2* Writing lesson (40 minutes)
- Modified Modeled and Independent Reading at seats (20 minutes)
- Wrap-Up (15 minutes)

Tip: As students complete the *RDI* lesson, have them get their materials for Modeled and Independent Reading and return to their seats to read.

Option 2:

- *RDI Book 1* Comprehension lesson or *RDI Book 2* Writing lesson (20 minutes)
- Students complete comprehension discussion questions or writing prompt independently while one group rotates to Instructional Software for 20 minutes at a time (60 minutes)
- Students who complete the lesson before their group is scheduled to go to Instructional Software can read their Modeled and Independent Reading book at their seats.
- Wrap-Up (10 minutes)

Tip: Designate one student per class to monitor the Topic Software CDs and make sure that they are put away in the appropriate place at the end of class.

Overview of *READ 180* for Substitute Teachers

Understanding *READ 180*

READ 180 is an intensive reading intervention program designed to meet the needs of students whose reading achievement is below the proficient level. The program directly addresses individual needs through adaptive, instructional software, high-interest literature, and direct instruction in reading and writing skills.

READ 180 Instructional Model

The *READ 180* Instructional Model provides a simple way to organize instruction and classroom activity. The session begins and ends with teacher-directed Whole-Group Instruction. In between Whole-Group meetings, students break into three small groups that rotate among three stations: *READ 180* Instructional Software, Small-Group Direct Instruction, and Modeled and Independent Reading.

READ 180 Classroom

READ 180 classroom is a special place for reading, learning, and sharing. You will find:

- Work tables or clusters of desks for teacher-directed **Small-Group Instruction**.
- A comfortable reading area for **Modeled and Independent Reading** with the *READ 180* Audiobooks and Paperbacks.
- A computer station for **Instructional Software** with the *READ 180* computer program.

READ 180 Core Program Components and Activities

Teacher Bookshelf

As a substitute teacher, you will mainly use items from the *Teacher's Edition* and *Resources for Differentiated Instruction* (RDI) books.

Student Materials

In the *READ 180* classroom, there will also be several items which students will need access to, including the Instructional Software, *READ 180* Paperbacks for independent reading, Audiobooks for modeled reading, and *rBooks*. These are interactive worktexts students use during Whole- and Small-Group Instruction, which provide daily instruction in reading comprehension, vocabulary, and writing and grammar skills.

Suggested Activities

- Whole Group: Select a lesson from RDI Book 1 (20 minutes)
- Modeled and Independent Reading: Students at this rotation can read independently in the reading area (20 minutes)
- Instructional Software: Students at this rotation should work on the *READ 180* software independently. They may be recording passages out loud (20 minutes)
- Small Group: Work with students on an RDI Book 2 writing lesson (20 minutes)
- Whole Group: Students come together to reflect on lessons learned (10 minutes)

Student Exit Criteria

Most schools set their own criteria to assess readiness to move beyond the *READ 180* classroom. Some exit students who reach a certain performance level, e.g., Proficient, those who are reading grade level text from the program. Students may also leave *READ 180* when changing schools or to make way for students with greatest need. Following are recommendations for evaluating readiness to exit *READ 180* and supporting students who make the transition.

Pacing and Differentiating

READ 180 students may have a wide range of skills and reading levels. As they respond to the program, students make gains at their own rates. Some accelerate through the Topic Software but take longer to increase their SRI Lexile scores. Others may be successful using the ***rBook*** during direct instruction but need more practice to transfer strategies they learned to independent reading or other classes.

Using Multiple Measures of Success

It is important to use multiple formal and informal measures to determine a student's readiness to leave the *READ 180* program. Formal measures may include increases in:

- Lexile scores (to grade level proficiency range).
- State/district standardized tests.
- SRI normative data (percentiles, NCEs, or Stanines).
- Scores on grade level *READ 180 rSkills Tests*.
- *READ 180* Topic Software data (e.g., context score and rate).
- ***rBook*** completion and success level.

Informal measures to look at may include:

- Observations of skill levels, motivation, attitude, and behavior.
- *Scholastic Reading Counts!* Quiz scores.
- Number and level of books read (or *Scholastic Reading Counts!* Quizzes passed).
- Ability to read and demonstrate comprehension independently.
- Student self-evaluations.

Supporting Students Beyond *READ 180*

When students leave *READ 180*, it is important to place them into supportive classrooms and monitor their progress as they encounter more difficult content and reading materials. To foster continued success after *READ 180*, encourage students to continue choosing books at the appropriate Lexile levels, especially for independent reading. Ideally students should leave the *READ 180* program at a regular break in the school year, such as at the end of a semester.

Planning *READ 180* Professional Development

Scholastic offers comprehensive *READ 180* implementation training and professional development to teachers to help them foster and sustain best teaching practices in the classroom.

- **Best Practices for Professional Development**
- ***READ 180* Implementation Training and Professional Development**
- **Red Pages in the *READ 180 Teacher's Edition***
- **Scholastic Red Routines**

Best Practices for Professional Development

Teachers who receive support and coaching generally practice new strategies more frequently and develop greater skill with teaching new strategies than teachers who do not receive the same type of support (Showers, 1982).

READ 180 Professional Development and Scholastic Red are research-based, comprehensive professional development solutions that improve teacher practice and raise student achievement in reading. They are ongoing to help teachers develop teaching strategies and offered in person as well as online, allowing districts and teachers to complete courses based on their schedules.

To truly succeed, a reading professional development program must incorporate six crucial elements. It must be:

1. Scientifically Research-Based

Theory and research on best instructional practices can stimulate reflection, discussion, and a direction for improving practices that increase student achievement. Scholastic Red professional development experiences are created by the Scholastic Red faculty—nationally recognized experts—and are based on validated instructional approaches.

2. Focused on Student Reading Achievement

The *READ 180* Seminar Series and Red courses are entirely focused on the goal of improving student reading achievement. The *READ 180* Seminar Series combine a research foundation with interactive activities designed to take teachers to the next level of success with *READ 180*. Red courses are proven to improve the quality of reading instruction, which leads to higher achievement in reading for all students.

> **"Effective professional development activities are sustained over a long period of time and carefully planned to provide early and ongoing feedback."**
> **—Ganser, 2000**

3. Systemic and Ongoing

READ 180 Seminar Series and Red courses ensure that teachers receive ongoing, in-depth professional development. Reading instruction improves continually through interactive activities designed to take teachers to the next level of success with *READ 180*.

4. Customizable to Meet District Needs

Every school district has its own unique set of challenges around reading and professional development. Scholastic Red works in partnership with school and district leaders to develop customized professional development solutions in reading that are tightly aligned to local standards, assessments, and instructional programs. Solutions can include online courses, on-site workshops, leadership institutes, and ongoing teacher and coach support—all designed to complement local professional development plans.

5. Aligned With Standards

Our courses meet standards for national accreditation and are designed to complement and support the ongoing work of district- and school-based staff developers. Scholastic Red works with district curriculum and professional development staff to write custom correlations of Red programs to core reading programs and standards.

6. Continuously Providing Teacher Support

Teachers have access to lesson plans, resources, professional articles, and Web links that connect to the course content and continue the support throughout the school year.

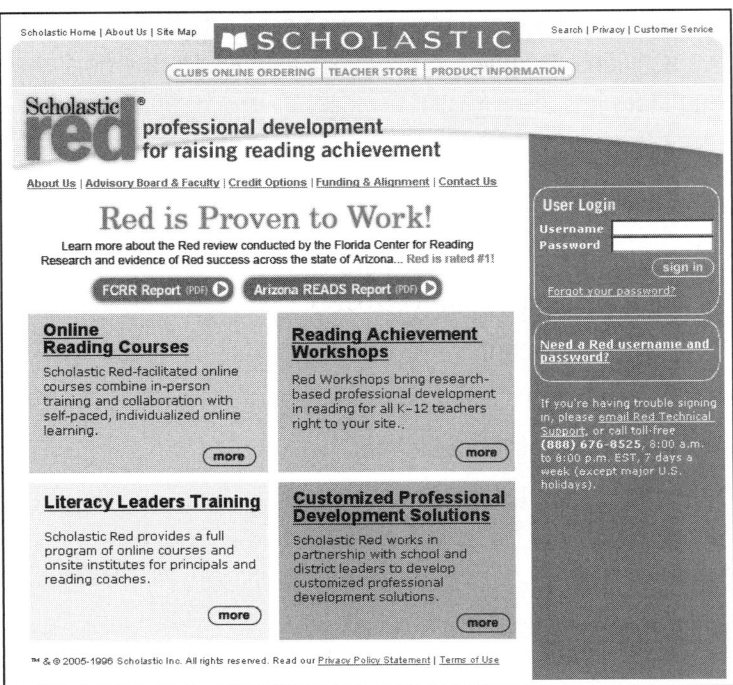

READ 180 Implementation Training and Professional Development

Scholastic offers a comprehensive professional development program to support *READ 180* educators and to raise student reading achievement. Courses are available online and/or in person. Present course offerings include:

READ 180 Implementation Training

Scholastic offers two days of in-person implementation training for teachers, and reading and literacy specialists to learn how to implement the *READ 180* Instructional Model and employ best practices with the program.

Leadership Training

Scholastic offers a three-hour on-site leadership training for administrators and principals. This training prepares leaders to build and support effective *READ 180* programs in their schools and districts.

Online Course: *READ 180*: Best Practices for Reading Intervention

An online course through Scholastic Red at **www.scholasticred.com** is designed to support implementing resources in a *READ 180* classroom. The seven sessions in this course focus on the latest research findings on the struggling reader, research-based teaching techniques, guidelines for effective use of the *READ 180* Software, and how to use *READ 180* assessment tools to guide instruction.

READ 180 Seminar Series

Scholastic offers the *READ 180* Seminar Series, eight half-day seminars that combine a research foundation with interactive activities designed to take your teachers to the next level of success with *READ 180*. Seminars include:

- Decoding Strategies for *READ 180* Students
- Developing Independent Readers in the *READ 180* Classroom
- Motivating the *READ 180* Student
- Strategic Comprehension and Vocabulary Instruction in *READ 180*
- Test-Taking Strategies for the *READ 180* Classroom
- Using *READ 180* Data to Differentiate Instruction
- Using SRI and the Lexile Framework Effectively With *READ 180*
- Writing in the Service of Reading for the *READ 180* Classroom

Facilitated Online Reading Courses

Graduate level online reading courses help teachers continue and deepen their professional development. These courses provide convenient, targeted training in differentiating instruction and increasing reading achievement for all students. These courses can be used in buildings or districts to support content-area teaching. Currently available online reading courses include:

- Building Decoding Skills and Strategies, Grades 3–5

- Guided Reading: Making It Work in Your Classroom, Grades K–6

- Improving Decoding Skills and Strategies, Grades 6–8

- Improving Fluency, Grades 3–8

- Improving Reading Comprehension, Grades 3–5

- Middle School Literacy: Improving Text Comprehension

- High School Literacy: Comprehension Through Active, Strategic Reading

Integrated Red Professional Development

The *READ 180 **rBook** Teacher's Edition, RDI* Books, and *Teaching Resources* guides include integrated professional development so that teachers receive the background, teaching routines, and instructional support they need. The following types of Red Professional Development are available in the ***rBook** Teacher's Edition:*

- Research Foundation Red Pages: These pages explain the big ideas and research behind *READ 180*, such as narrow reading and adaptive technology.

- Instructional Routines Red Pages: These pages provide background and procedures for teaching and using recursive instructional routines, such as Oral Cloze and Think (Write)-Pair-Share.

- Best Practices Red Pages: These pages provide teachers with the rationale and resources for teaching specific comprehension skills, such as summarizing and sequence of events.

- Using SAM Reports Red Pages: These pages direct teachers on how to use report data from the *Scholastic Achievement Manager* (SAM) to differentiate and individualize instruction.

- Classroom Management: These columns located within the Differentiated Support at the end of each Workshop offer practical ideas for *READ 180* teaching and implementation, such as how to group and regroup students for instruction.

More information on Red Pages in the ***rBook** Teacher's Edition* are included on the following pages. Teachers can use Red pages for ongoing background and support. Reading coaches can also use them as a focus for cadre meetings or study groups for *READ 180* teachers.

Red Pages in the *READ 180 Teacher's Edition*

The *Teacher's Edition* provides teaching support through integrated, point-of-use professional development, as well as routines and research for reference throughout the year.

Red pages present research-based information in a teacher-friendly format.

Background information and rationale explain the *what* and the *why,* as well as the *how* of using each routine.

Step-by-step instructions for routines include sample teacher-modeling. Routines may be used flexibly within the *READ 180* teaching system and in other subject areas.

INSTRUCTIONAL ROUTINE: Teaching Vocabulary

What Research Says
- Planned and explicit vocabulary instruction is essential to support students' comprehension (Feldman & Kinsella, 2004).
- Students learn new vocabulary when it is taught using a consistent instructional sequence (Feldman & Kinsella, 2004).

Why It's Important
- Builds background knowledge for reading
- Increases ability to understand text
- Bolsters speaking and listening skills

How to Do It
- Follow the vocabulary teaching routine throughout a Workshop when you introduce Target Words.

> *Direct vocabulary instruction that includes high-incidence academic words yields a great return because students will repeatedly encounter these words throughout reading in content areas and across the grades.*
>
> **Dr. Kate Kinsella**

Red Routine ❶

Teaching Vocabulary

Follow this engaging routine to teach the academic vocabulary needed to comprehend text and discuss content.

What Is the Vocabulary Routine?

Academic vocabulary includes the high-utility words that students will encounter across the content areas (e.g., *analysis, consequence*), along with words necessary to build background for specific concepts (e.g., *volcanic, Patriot*). The Teaching Vocabulary routine is a step-by-step way to make new academic words meaningful. The words essential for comprehension are called "Target Words" in the *rBooks* and appear repeatedly throughout reading passages.

Why Use the Vocabulary Routine?

Teaching students carefully selected words using a consistent sequence will help them build background knowledge essential for comprehension (Feldman & Kinsella, 2004). When students encounter unfamiliar words, they often rely on the teacher to provide on-the-spot support, which interrupts reading and can limit comprehension. Teaching words before they cause difficulty allows students to engage in fluent and confident reading.

Rating Vocabulary Knowledge

Before teaching new vocabulary, have students evaluate their knowledge of the words using the rating scale provided in the *rBook.* This allows students to activate prior knowledge and identify confusing words. This helps you assess students' background knowledge and prioritize words during instruction.

❶ **Set purpose** by explaining that students will rate and learn words from their upcoming readings.
Rating words and thinking about what you already know will help you better understand the reading.

❷ **Read** and rate each Target Word.
How well do you know this word? If you don't know it at all, rate it a 1. If you have seen or heard it before, rate it a 2. If you know it and can use it, rate it a 3.

❸ **Discuss** students' prior knowledge of the words.

How to Use the Teaching Vocabulary Routine

❶ **Pronounce** the word and ask students to repeat it. Then give the part of speech. For example:
The word is fierce. Repeat after me: fierce. Fierce an adjective, or a describing word.

❷ **Explain** the meaning of the word using the explanation provided in this book. Record it Transparency 1 and have students complete their *rBooks.* Then, rephrase the definition, ing students to complete it by substituting t Target Word chorally.
Something that is fierce is angry and violent. Wri this meaning for fierce in your rBook.
Something that is angry and violent is _____ (fie

❸ **Discuss** at least two meaningful examples, record them on **Transparency 1,** and have students complete them in their *rBooks.* Th have students generate their own examples. Model examples and additional ideas are provided in this book.

❹ **Ask** the question provided in this book to de en understanding. Coach students to use the Target Word and respond in complete senten to explain their views.
How can you tell if an animal is fierce?

❺ **Review** all of the Target Words by having students work together to complete the sente starters provided in this book.
You should be cautious of growling dogs off a lea because they may be very _____! (fierce)

T72) **READ 180** Professional Development

Classroom-tested strategies provide support to promote success in using routines with struggling readers.

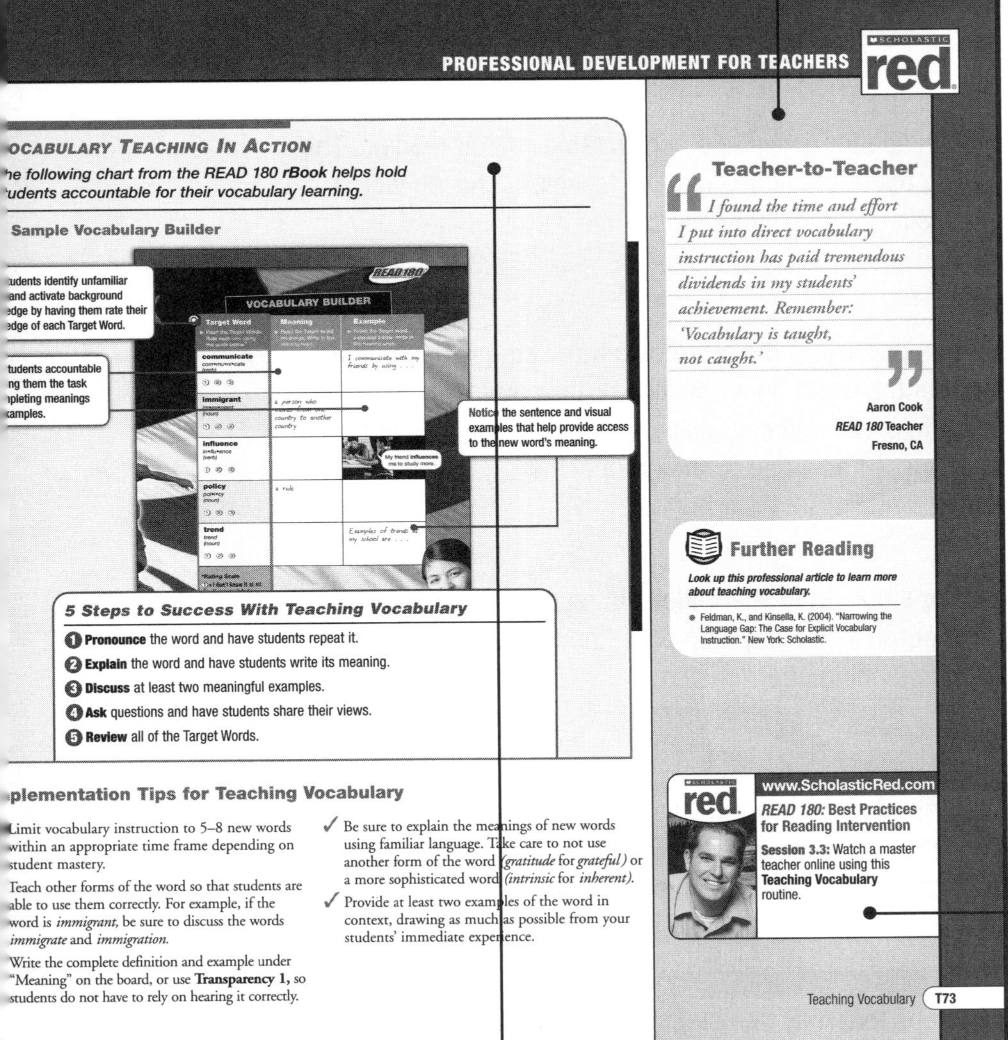

PROFESSIONAL DEVELOPMENT FOR TEACHERS   SCHOLASTIC red.

VOCABULARY TEACHING IN ACTION

The following chart from the READ 180 rBook helps hold students accountable for their vocabulary learning.

Sample Vocabulary Builder

Students identify unfamiliar and activate background knowledge by having them rate their knowledge of each Target Word.

Students accountable by giving them the task of completing meanings and examples.

READ 180
VOCABULARY BUILDER

Target Word | Meaning | Example
communicate | | I communicate with my friends by using . . .
immigrant | a person who moves from one country to another country |
influence | | My friend influences me to study more.
policy | a rule |
trend | | Examples of trends in my school are . . .

Notice the sentence and visual examples that help provide access to the new word's meaning.

5 Steps to Success With Teaching Vocabulary

1 Pronounce the word and have students repeat it.
2 Explain the word and have students write its meaning.
3 Discuss at least two meaningful examples.
4 Ask questions and have students share their views.
5 Review all of the Target Words.

Implementation Tips for Teaching Vocabulary

Limit vocabulary instruction to 5–8 new words within an appropriate time frame depending on student mastery.

Teach other forms of the word so that students are able to use them correctly. For example, if the word is immigrant, be sure to discuss the words immigrate and immigration.

Write the complete definition and example under "Meaning" on the board, or use Transparency 1, so students do not have to rely on hearing it correctly.

✓ Be sure to explain the meanings of new words using familiar language. Take care to not use another form of the word (gratitude for grateful) or a more sophisticated word (intrinsic for inherent).

✓ Provide at least two examples of the word in context, drawing as much as possible from your students' immediate experience.

Teacher-to-Teacher

" I found the time and effort I put into direct vocabulary instruction has paid tremendous dividends in my students' achievement. Remember: 'Vocabulary is taught, not caught.' "

Aaron Cook
READ 180 Teacher
Fresno, CA

Further Reading

Look up this professional article to learn more about teaching vocabulary.

• Feldman, K., and Kinsella, K. (2004). "Narrowing the Language Gap: The Case for Explicit Vocabulary Instruction." New York: Scholastic.

red   www.ScholasticRed.com

READ 180: Best Practices for Reading Intervention

Session 3.3: Watch a master teacher online using this Teaching Vocabulary routine.

Teaching Vocabulary   T73

The online READ 180 Red course provides additional information in a multimedia format.

Specific examples show research and procedures in context.

"Active participation of all students is absolutely essential to the success of every lesson. This is especially the case in today's diverse classrooms, with a range of learners and skill levels."
—Dr. Kevin Feldman

Scholastic Red Routines

READ 180 Red Routines provide research-based teaching protocols that teachers can learn easily and practice repeatedly to ensure that their instruction is consistent and effective. Using Red Routines for vocabulary, writing, and other areas, helps students know what to expect, how to respond, and how they will be held accountable for learning.

Teaching Vocabulary

The Teaching Vocabulary routine is a step-by-step strategy to make new academic words meaningful. The words essential for comprehension are called "Target Words" in the *rBooks* and appear repeatedly throughout reading passages.

Oral Cloze

Oral Cloze is a research-based technique for active and accountable shared reading. The teacher reads a text aloud, modeling fluent reading, and omits specially chosen words. Students are directed to read along silently and chime in with the words omitted.

Think (Write)-Pair-Share

Think (Write)-Pair-Share is a low-risk partnering structure with three stages of student interaction. First, students independently reflect on a question or task and write their ideas down. Next, partners discuss their ideas with accountability for sharing and listening. Finally, students present the ideas they discussed as a pair to the group.

Idea Wave

Idea Wave is a structured method for students to share ideas in response to a focused question or task before or after reading. The purpose is to tap into prior knowledge before reading or to synthesize and elaborate upon understanding after reading.

Numbered Heads

Students learn more from discussions when they are held accountable for participating and listening actively. Numbered Heads is a cooperative-learning routine that structures small groups for discussions or for tasks, making sure that all members are prepared to share.

Writing Process

The Writing Process is a series of steps that may be used in the course of developing a piece of writing. The *READ 180* **rBook** focuses on teaching several writing types using the Writing Process so that students internalize key text structures as well as the steps to follow for writing.

Peer Feedback

Peer Feedback is a writing revision strategy in which two students work together using a scoring guide, or rubric, to evaluate the content and organization of their drafts.

Assessing and Reporting with *READ 180*

The *READ 180* Software begins collecting data about students from the moment they log on. SAM, the Scholastic Achievement Manager, uses this data to generate reports about students, classes, schools, and districts. *READ 180* reports provide detailed information about students' progress in fluency, word study, vocabulary, comprehension, and spelling. They can facilitate your administrative and management tasks.

- *READ 180* **Assessment Time Line**
- **Using SAM to Support Accountability and AYP Targets**
- *READ 180* **Participation Summary Report**
- **SRI Proficiency Growth Report**
- **SRI Demographic Proficiency Report**
- *rSkills Tests* **Summary Skills Report**

READ 180 Assessment Time Line

This time line recommends when to administer appropriate placement, diagnostic, curriculum-based, and progress monitoring assessments to *READ 180* students over the course of a school year.

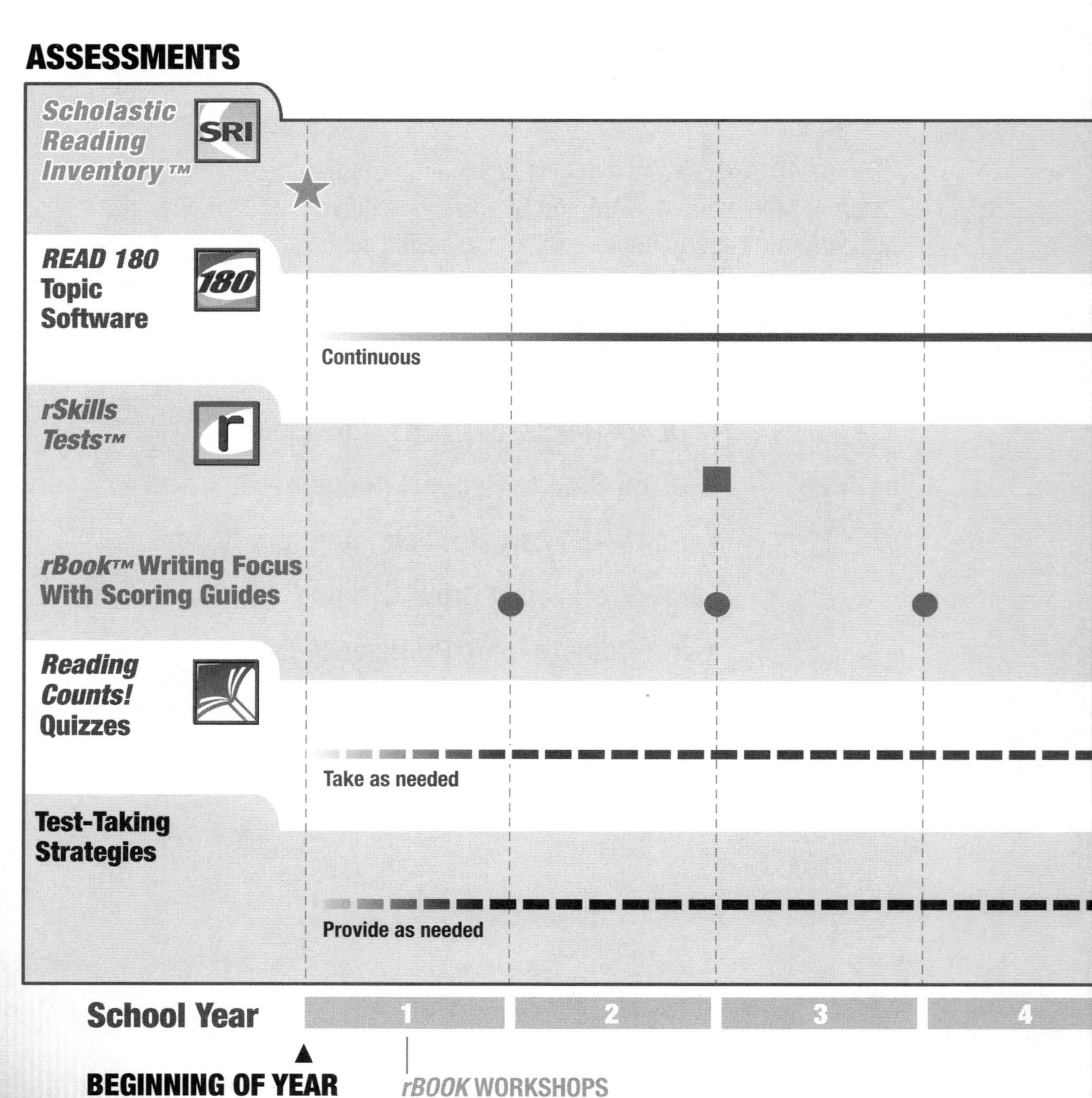

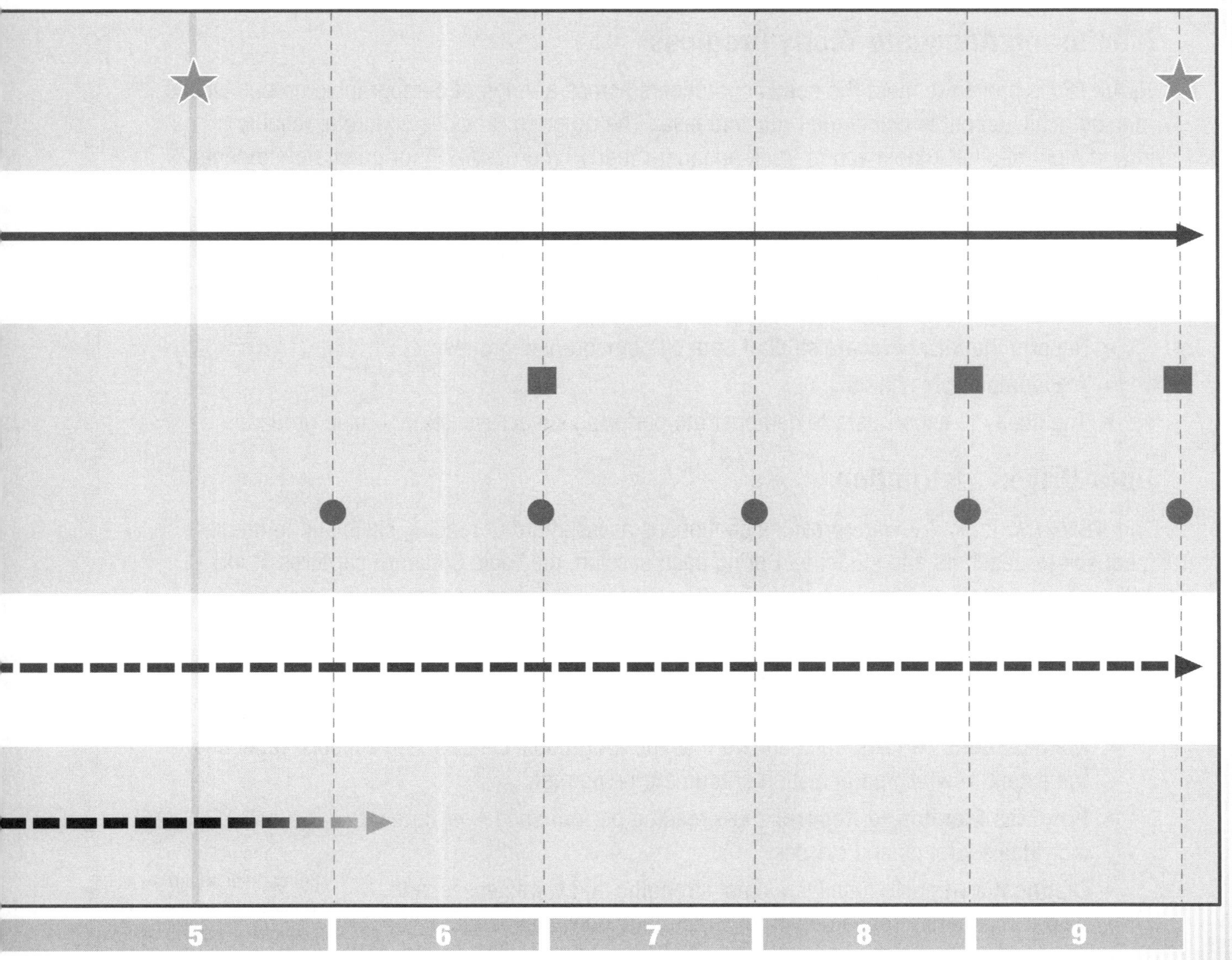

TYPES OF ASSESSMENT IN READ 180
Screening, Placement, and Progress Monitoring
Scholastic Reading Inventory
Continuous Diagnostic
READ 180 Topic Software
Curriculum-Based
rSkills Tests
rBook Writing Focus With Scoring Guides
Progress Monitoring
Reading Counts! Quizzes
Test-Taking Strategies
5
6
7
8
9
MID YEAR
END OF YEAR

Using SAM to Support Accountability and AYP Targets

As students participate in *READ 180*, the *Scholastic Achievement Manager* (SAM) captures important data that enables you to monitor the effectiveness of program implementation in your school or district. You can access this information using a variety of reports from the *READ 180* Software, *rSkills Tests*, Scholastic Reading Inventory (SRI) and *Scholastic Reading Counts!*

Using this information, you will be able to track program usage and reading progress for classes, grades, groups, schools, or teachers to ensure that students in your district are getting the maximum benefits from *READ 180* and its accompanying Scholastic programs.

Monitoring Adequate Yearly Progress

READ 180 is proven to meet the needs of students across a range of demographic groups whose reading achievement is below the proficient level. The program provides concrete, reliable information that will enable you to track Adequate Yearly Progress (AYP) for groups of students across a school or district.

More specifically, to help you meet AYP requirements in your state, *READ 180* offers:
- A reliable mechanism for monitoring, evaluating, and reporting progress.
- Differentiated instruction to meet unique student needs.
- Reports that disaggregate student data by demographic groups.
- AYP demographic filters.
- The ability to export data to demonstrate performance across demographic groups.

Data-Driven Instruction

The *READ 180* Topic Software provides continuous assessment of reading skills and immediate feedback for teachers and students. During each session, the Topic Software captures student software usage and performance data. Teachers can use the data from computer-generated reports to target instruction in ways that enable students to improve their performance.

READ 180 offers a variety of reports to help you monitor student achievement and meet AYP goals in your school or district.
- **Management Reports** track software usage for groups, classes, and schools, reflecting the extent to which participation criteria are being met.
- **Progress Monitoring Reports** show reading performance over time for individuals, groups and classes.
- **Diagnostic Reports** detail students' strengths and weaknesses, and help teachers differentiate instruction to meet individual needs.
- **Instructional Planning Reports** help teachers plan targeted, data-driven instruction for Whole and Small Groups.

"The ability to aggregate district data as well as to drill down to individualized student data is extremely valuable for instruction decision-making."
—Kim Eaton, District Technical Curriculum Coordinator, Ohio

READ 180 Participation Summary Report

Purpose Use this report to compare *READ 180* performance progress for schools or groups.

Follow-Up Run this report at the end of each grading period to track reading levels within a school or district.

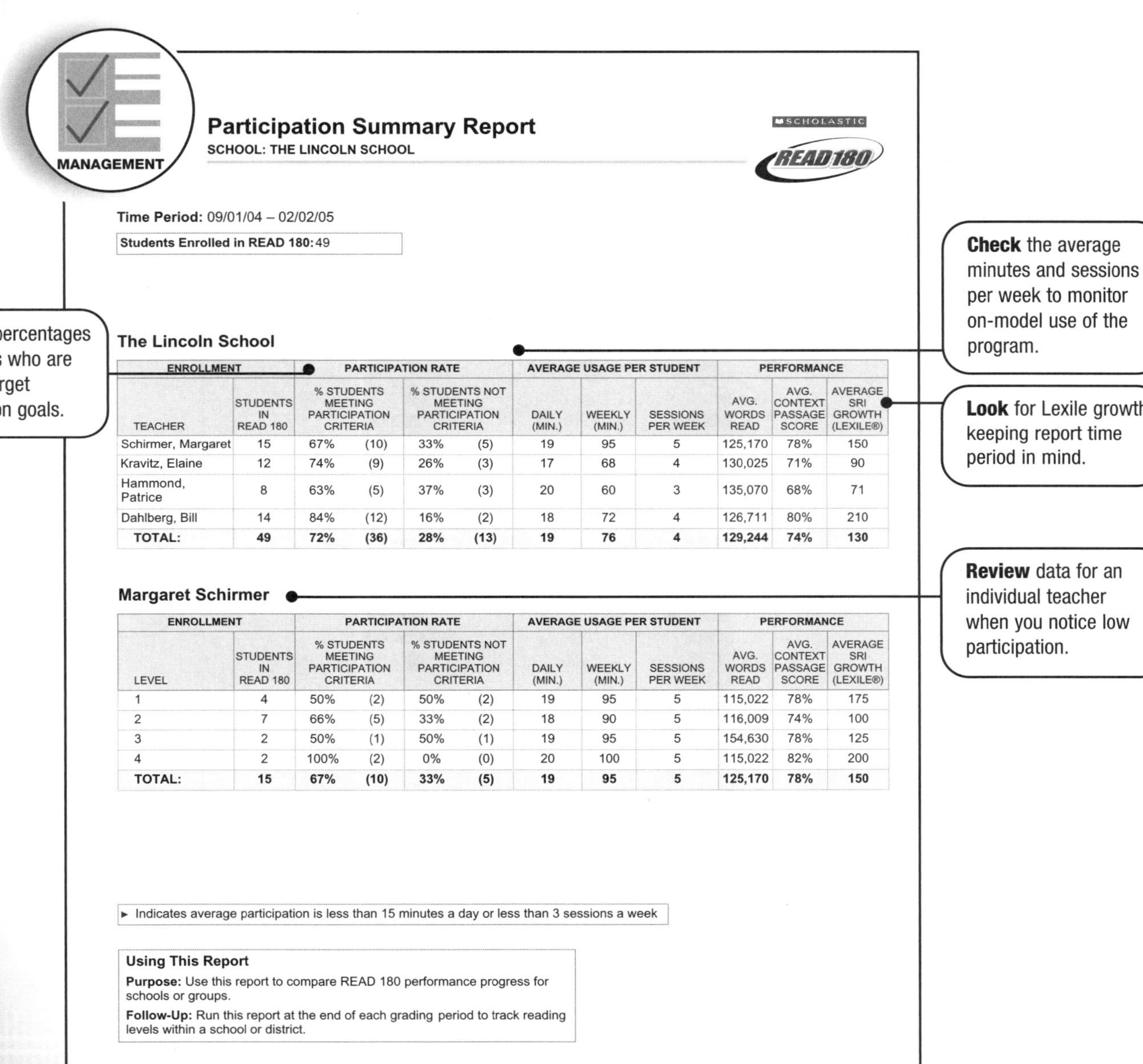

Participation Summary Report
SCHOOL: THE LINCOLN SCHOOL

■SCHOLASTIC
READ 180

MANAGEMENT

Time Period: 09/01/04 – 02/02/05

Students Enrolled in READ 180: 49

The Lincoln School

ENROLLMENT		PARTICIPATION RATE				AVERAGE USAGE PER STUDENT			PERFORMANCE		
TEACHER	STUDENTS IN READ 180	% STUDENTS MEETING PARTICIPATION CRITERIA		% STUDENTS NOT MEETING PARTICIPATION CRITERIA		DAILY (MIN.)	WEEKLY (MIN.)	SESSIONS PER WEEK	AVG. WORDS READ	AVG. CONTEXT PASSAGE SCORE	AVERAGE SRI GROWTH (LEXILE®)
Schirmer, Margaret	15	67%	(10)	33%	(5)	19	95	5	125,170	78%	150
Kravitz, Elaine	12	74%	(9)	26%	(3)	17	68	4	130,025	71%	90
Hammond, Patrice	8	63%	(5)	37%	(3)	20	60	3	135,070	68%	71
Dahlberg, Bill	14	84%	(12)	16%	(2)	18	72	4	126,711	80%	210
TOTAL:	**49**	**72%**	**(36)**	**28%**	**(13)**	**19**	**76**	**4**	**129,244**	**74%**	**130**

Margaret Schirmer

ENROLLMENT		PARTICIPATION RATE				AVERAGE USAGE PER STUDENT			PERFORMANCE		
LEVEL	STUDENTS IN READ 180	% STUDENTS MEETING PARTICIPATION CRITERIA		% STUDENTS NOT MEETING PARTICIPATION CRITERIA		DAILY (MIN.)	WEEKLY (MIN.)	SESSIONS PER WEEK	AVG. WORDS READ	AVG. CONTEXT PASSAGE SCORE	AVERAGE SRI GROWTH (LEXILE®)
1	4	50%	(2)	50%	(2)	19	95	5	115,022	78%	175
2	7	66%	(5)	33%	(2)	18	90	5	116,009	74%	100
3	2	50%	(1)	50%	(1)	19	95	5	154,630	78%	125
4	2	100%	(2)	0%	(0)	20	100	5	115,022	82%	200
TOTAL:	**15**	**67%**	**(10)**	**33%**	**(5)**	**19**	**95**	**5**	**125,170**	**78%**	**150**

▶ Indicates average participation is less than 15 minutes a day or less than 3 sessions a week

Using This Report

Purpose: Use this report to compare READ 180 performance progress for schools or groups.

Follow-Up: Run this report at the end of each grading period to track reading levels within a school or district.

How It Helps

"This report is a great way to get an overview of schools and classes that are making good use of READ 180. *It's encouraging to see positive results from month to month!"*

SRI Proficiency Growth Report

Purpose This report shows changes in distribution across performance standards over time by district, school, grade, and teacher.

Follow-Up Identify schools (or grades within a school, or classes for individual teachers) that are not showing adequate growth over time, and provide extra help to optimize SRI performance.

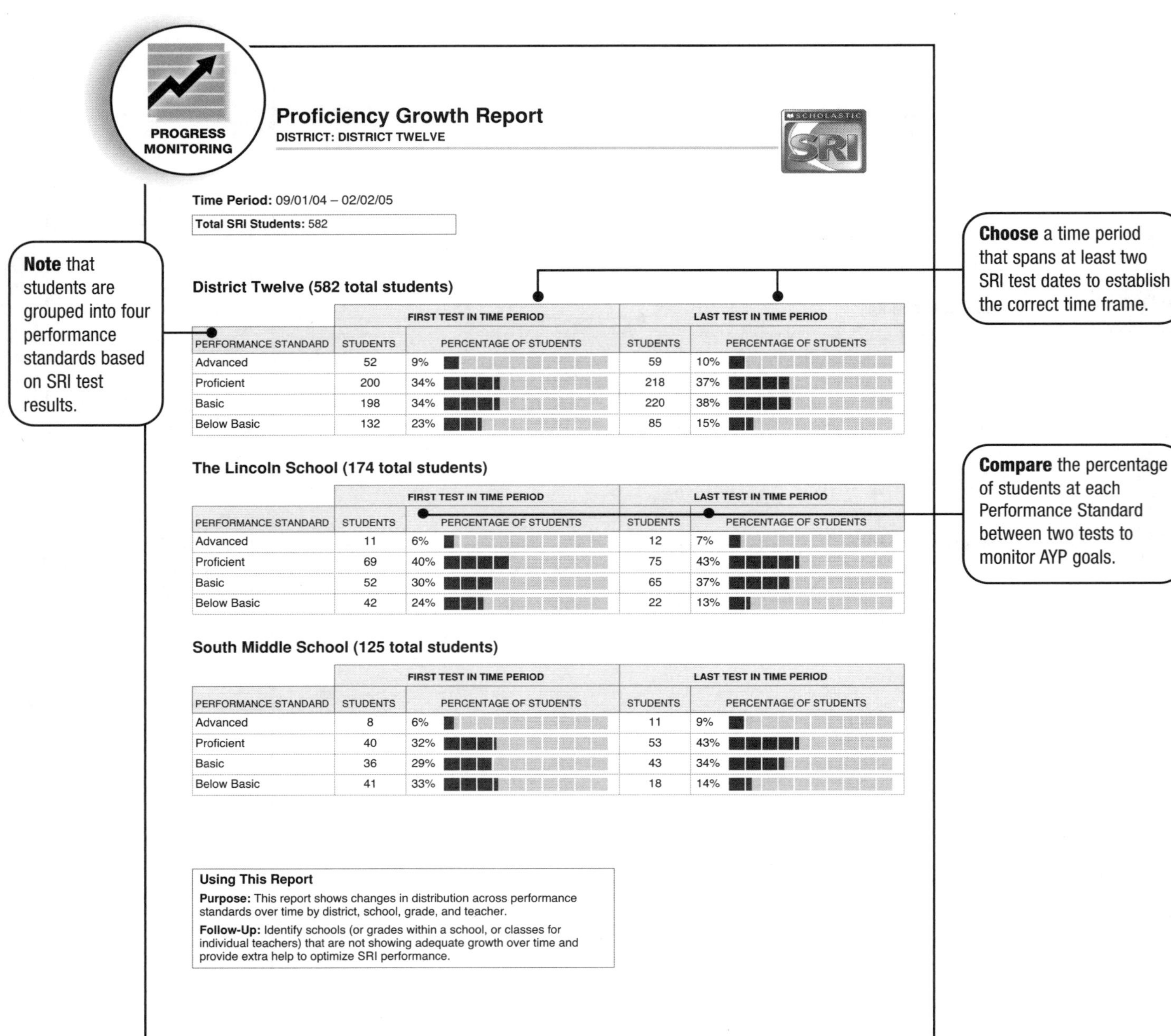

PERFORMANCE STANDARD	STUDENTS	FIRST TEST IN TIME PERIOD PERCENTAGE OF STUDENTS	STUDENTS	LAST TEST IN TIME PERIOD PERCENTAGE OF STUDENTS
Advanced	52	9%	59	10%
Proficient	200	34%	218	37%
Basic	198	34%	220	38%
Below Basic	132	23%	85	15%

PERFORMANCE STANDARD	STUDENTS	FIRST TEST IN TIME PERIOD PERCENTAGE OF STUDENTS	STUDENTS	LAST TEST IN TIME PERIOD PERCENTAGE OF STUDENTS
Advanced	11	6%	12	7%
Proficient	69	40%	75	43%
Basic	52	30%	65	37%
Below Basic	42	24%	22	13%

PERFORMANCE STANDARD	STUDENTS	FIRST TEST IN TIME PERIOD PERCENTAGE OF STUDENTS	STUDENTS	LAST TEST IN TIME PERIOD PERCENTAGE OF STUDENTS
Advanced	8	6%	11	9%
Proficient	40	32%	53	43%
Basic	36	29%	43	34%
Below Basic	41	33%	18	14%

Note that students are grouped into four performance standards based on SRI test results.

Choose a time period that spans at least two SRI test dates to establish the correct time frame.

Compare the percentage of students at each Performance Standard between two tests to monitor AYP goals.

How It Helps

"I use this report to track reading performance by district and school between two points in time. I can monitor progress and assess whether my district is meeting AYP accountability requirements."

SRI Demographic Proficiency Report

Purpose This report provides a breakdown of SRI performance.

Follow-Up Identify demographic groups that are in need of extra help based on SRI performance standard percentages.

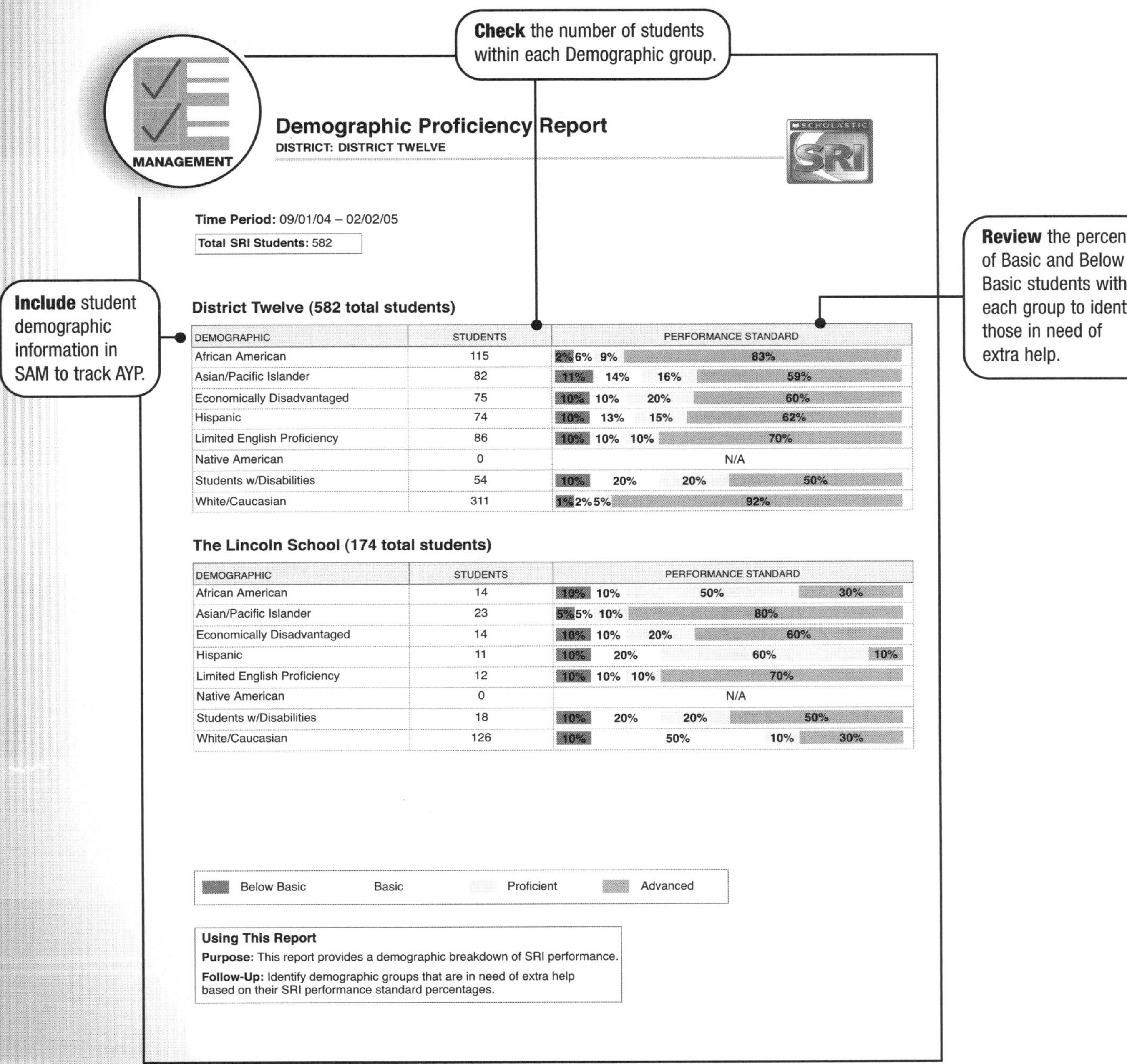

How It Helps

> *The Demographic Proficiency Report gives me data on demographic groups within my district. This information enables me to monitor progress toward meeting AYP requirements.*

rSkills Tests Summary Skills Report

Purpose This report shows aggregate *rSkills Tests* scores on one test for a class or group. The skill-by-skill score breakdown shows strengths and weaknesses.

Follow-Up Target specific skills for Whole- and Small-Group Instruction that a majority of your students are having difficulty with.

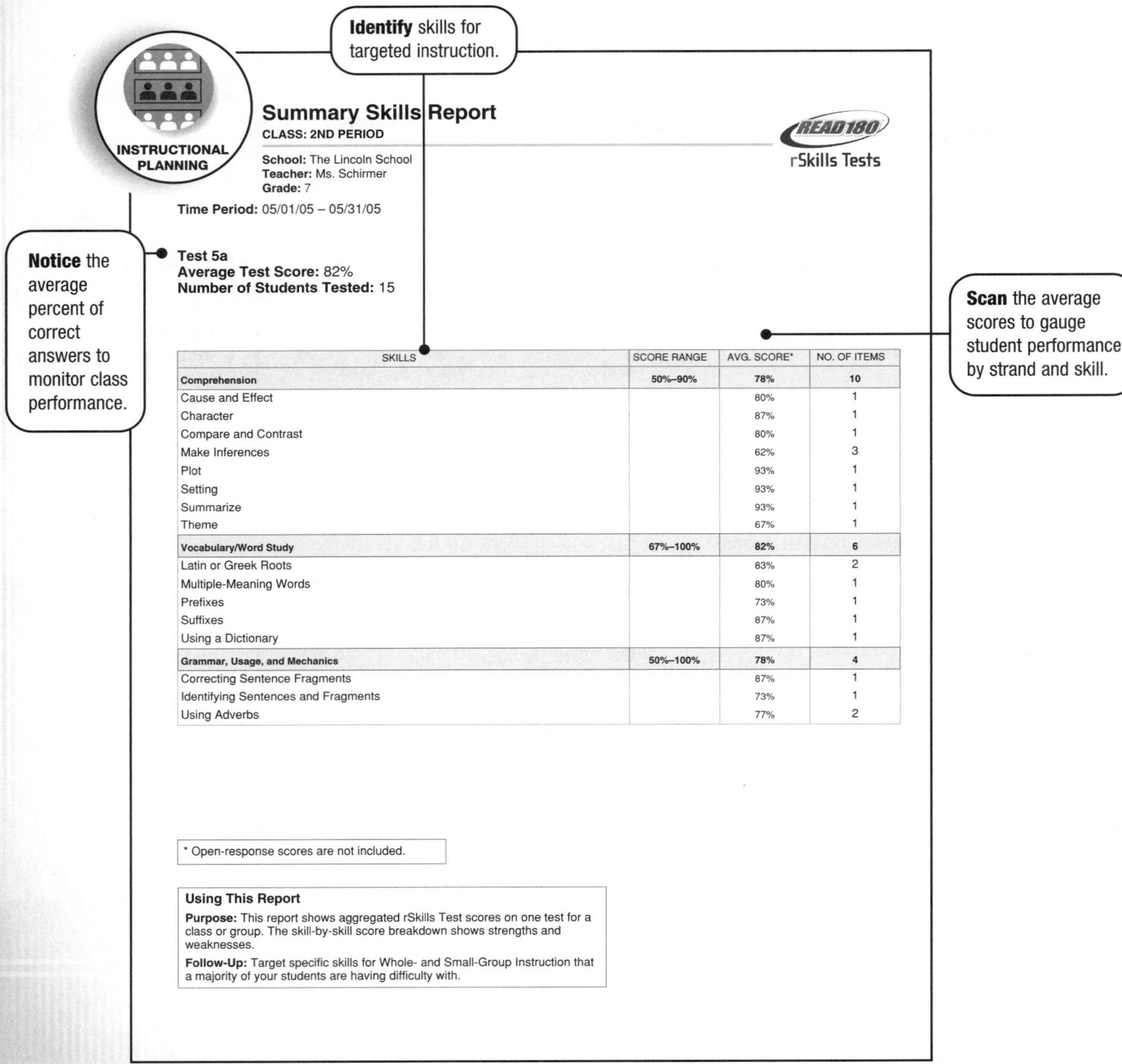

SKILLS	SCORE RANGE	AVG. SCORE*	NO. OF ITEMS
Comprehension	**50%–90%**	**78%**	**10**
Cause and Effect		80%	1
Character		87%	1
Compare and Contrast		80%	1
Make Inferences		62%	3
Plot		93%	1
Setting		93%	1
Summarize		93%	1
Theme		67%	1
Vocabulary/Word Study	**67%–100%**	**82%**	**6**
Latin or Greek Roots		83%	2
Multiple-Meaning Words		80%	1
Prefixes		73%	1
Suffixes		87%	1
Using a Dictionary		87%	1
Grammar, Usage, and Mechanics	**50%–100%**	**78%**	**4**
Correcting Sentence Fragments		87%	1
Identifying Sentences and Fragments		73%	1
Using Adverbs		77%	2

* Open-response scores are not included.

Using This Report

Purpose: This report shows aggregated rSkills Test scores on one test for a class or group. The skill-by-skill score breakdown shows strengths and weaknesses.

Follow-Up: Target specific skills for Whole- and Small-Group Instruction that a majority of your students are having difficulty with.

> **How It Helps**
>
> **"** *This report provides an overview of students' ability to apply the skills they learn during Whole- and Small-Group Instruction. This information helps me to assess the effectiveness of teacher-directed instruction.* **"**

Making *READ 180* Community Connections

READ 180 provides resources and tools to facilitate communication between administrators, teachers, parents, and students.

- **Involving Families in *READ 180***
- **Welcome Letter for *READ 180* Families**
- **Frequently Asked Questions About *READ 180***
- **Administrator Resources**

Involving Families in *READ 180*

Getting Parents Involved

Here are some tips and suggestions for encouraging parental involvement in *READ 180* classes:

- **Encourage Modeling Behavior** Parents model what good readers do by reading and providing a literacy-rich environment by placing books throughout the house.

- **Reading at Home** Encourage parents to read to their child every day. Offer parent evenings on the best ways for parents to read books to their children.

- **Invite Parents Into the Classroom** Invite parents to read to their child's class and keep a photo album of each parent reading to the class.

- **Get to Know Parents and Children** Teachers can get to know parents and their children by sending them an invitation to write and "tell me about your child."

- **Establish a Book Loan Program** Establish a book loan program in the classroom or school. Research has shown that children will read more if they are allowed to choose their own titles and if they have a large number of books from which to choose.

- **Make a Class Web Page** Create a class Web page to keep parents apprised of what's happening in their child's classroom.

- **Host a *READ 180* Parent Night** Hold a *READ 180* Parent Night, explaining the *READ 180* program. Let parents participate in each of the *READ 180* rotations.

Supporting Reading in the Home

Here are some things parents can do at home to help children become lifelong readers:

- **The Daily Read** Make reading a daily activity by reading to, or with, your child for 20 minutes every day.

- **Fast and Fun Reads** Use magazines, newspapers, comic books, recipes, TV schedules, travel guides, and road signs as reading opportunities, wherever you are and whatever you and your child are doing.

- **The Movie or the Book** Rent videos or DVDs on a topic that your child is interested in. Find books on a similar topic.

- **Read and Ride** Listen to books on tape or CD while traveling by car. Bring a personal audio player with headphones for your child to listen to books while on a train or plane.

- **Read and Chat** Talk about what your child is reading. Ask questions about the characters or what happens in the story.

> "A lot of students who are not in the program want to be in the program. Kids are talking it up on the playground."
> —Tracy Topoleski,
> At Risk
> Intervention Teacher

Welcome Letter For *READ 180* Families

Send family letters home to introduce the program. Use this letter to introduce *READ 180* to parents and caregivers. Customize the sample letter to meet your particular district or schools needs.

Date: _________________

Dear Family,

Thousands of struggling students across the country experience frustration and lack of success in reading. In response to this problem, we selected Scholastic's *READ 180*, a groundbreaking intervention program proven to improve reading achievement for students who are reading below grade level. *READ 180* uses cutting-edge technology to deliver individualized reading instruction, provide valuable skills practice, and motivate students to become confident, successful readers.

Your child is currently enrolled in *READ 180* in our reading class. Together we will be working to:

- build essential literacy skills.

- bring his or her reading up to grade level.

- read at least 25 books this year.

- show your child that he or she can attain reading success

- apply those new literacy skills to other subjects such as social studies, math, and science.

Your child will need to work hard and will need your encouragement. Supporting reading at home will help your child become a lifelong reader. Visiting the library, setting aside reading time, and discussing the books your child reads will foster reading success. Thank you in advance for helping us achieve our goals.

Your Student's Reading Teacher,

____

Frequently Asked Questions About *READ 180*

What is *READ 180*?

READ 180 is a reading intervention program designed to meet the needs of students whose reading achievement is below the proficient level based on standardized test scores.

How are students selected for *READ 180*?

Students who score at the Basic or Below Basic levels in reading on standardized tests or other comparable measures are prime candidates for *READ 180* because they have the greatest potential for accelerated growth. *READ 180* utilizes the Lexile Framework to determine student reading levels and match students to appropriate texts. The Scholastic Reading Inventory is the primary placement tool for *READ 180*.

Why are *READ 180* classes 90 minutes in length?

READ 180 is a 90-minute program: 20 minutes for Whole-Group Instruction, 20 minutes for Small-Group Instruction, 20 minutes for individualized adaptive Instructional Software at computers, 20 minutes of Modeled and Independent Reading with leveled Paperbacks and Audiobooks, and 10 minutes for review and wrap-up. Unless *READ 180* is implemented as a full 90-minute program, research has shown that it is not possible to get the results that can be achieved through an on-model 90-minute implementation.

How will *READ 180* help students?

Reading and understanding history, science, even math textbooks requires much more than phonics and decoding—it also requires academic literacy skills such as critical thinking, inferential comprehension, and dealing with a variety of text patterns and organizational structures. Students in the Basic and Below Basic range should receive direct instruction in academic literacy so they may become more productive when reading and learning from textbooks in the core content areas.

How does *READ 180* help students acquire academic literacy?

READ 180 classes are limited in size for personalized instruction. Standards-based reading and writing is explicitly taught during Whole-Group Instruction, with direct application of these skills and strategies during Small-Group Instruction. High-interest literature is presented on Paperbacks and Audiobooks during Modeled and Independent Reading time. Individualized, adaptive Instructional Software features build background knowledge, vocabulary, word structures, spelling, comprehension, and proofreading skills. Students receive regular feedback and reports on their progress.

Administrator Resources

Scholastic Administrator Home Page

Use the Scholastic Administrator Home Page to find resources to improve professional development and classroom practice, find best practices from other schools, gain information about funding, see how other districts are using technology, discover leadership information, and stay up to date on government policies. Find it at http://www.scholastic.com/administrator/

Administrator Magazine

Scholastic Administr@tor is published eight times a year and includes insight into effective technology and leadership strategies used by leading school districts around the nation. *Scholastic Administr@tor* covers a wide range of critical and timely issues—including assessment, funding, appropriate uses of technology, professional development, and online learning. Look for your copy delivered free to all school districts in the country.

Scholastic Achievement Manager Resources

Remember that you can also use the *Scholastic Achievement Manager*, or SAM, to locate instructional resources to improve professional development and monitor the implementation of *READ 180*.

SAM provides access to a variety of instructional resources that teachers and administrators can use to enhance the effectiveness of *READ 180*. Resources can be used:

- for the classroom: lessons, graphic organizers, and passages

- for individual students: practice pages, BLMs, speed drills, certificates, homework, *READ 180* rubrics, *READ 180* QuickWrites, and passages

- for professional development: professional articles, Scholastic Research Reports, Scholastic Red professional development course previews, and funding grant tool kits

- for implementation: classroom management forms and software manuals

We are grateful to the members of our Inaugural Implementation Advisory Board for their ideas, feedback, and support:

Jana Abshire, Director of Title 1 Programs,
City of Hammond, Indiana

Niki Bates, *READ 180* Coordinator,
Clark County School District, Nevada

Kim Eaton, District Technology Curriculum Coordinator,
Fairfield School District, Ohio

Dr. Peggy Gordon, Associate Superintendent for Middle Schools,
Independent School District, Texas

Maureen Harris, Assistant Director of Curriculum and Instructional Practices,
Boston Public Schools, Massachusetts

Diane Harazin, Curriculum Technology Specialist,
Fairfax County Public Schools, Virginia

June Jones, *READ 180* Coordinator,
Pinellas County Schools, Florida

Mike Rosenberg, Principal,
Grover Washington Middle School, Pennsylvania

Ann Shufflebarger, K–12 Remediation Coordinator,
Virginia Beach City Schools, Virginia

Jeanette Thomas, Communications Arts Facilitator,
Kirkwood School District, Missouri

Dr. Joe Witt, Professor and Director of Louisiana State University Behavior
Intervention Team, Louisiana

Dr. Miyo Chun, Professor of Decision Sciences,
Louisiana State University, Louisiana